8 SHORT STORIES

D0326041

Wayne J. Landry

Sally Guillot Bourgeois
Thanks for your help and encouragement.

CONTENTS

AMERICAN HERO/ AMERICAN VILLAIN

She could feel the sun's warmth on her velvety butterfly wings. Everything around her was so bright and colorful. She couldn't believe how easy it was to fly or float in the gentle breeze. Everything was perfect except the persistent slightly irritating droning sound in the background. Suddenly her mind shifted to recognition. She quickly sat up and reached for her phone to switch off the alarm. Her dreams were usually beautiful fantasies; her reality was a boring bitch. She laid back down to get that perfect early morning stretch and thought about how routine her day was going to be. As usual that last bit of bed relaxation felt so comforting, that delicious sleep which felt like one minute or maybe two at the most turned into thirty minutes of warm bliss. A peek from under the quilt, her eyes straining to adjust, she couldn't believe the damn clock was telling her it was already seven thirty. She'd better get up because her cameraman, Snowy, would soon be knocking on her door. Before she could get her feet on the floor there was a knock on the door. She sat on the side of the bed concentrating, trying to remember when she told Snowy to drive her to her next assignment. Stretching her arms over her head she looked into the spy hole and there was Snowy, her albino cameraman. She opened the door, motioned for him to enter and in her hoarse morning voice said, "What the hell are you doing here so early?"

Wide awake and all smiles, Snowy walked into the warm and cozy apartment. "Early! We need to be on site for nine o'clock. It'll take us at least thirty minutes to get there and you did say come over between seven thirty and eight. I'm on time eager for the day and your ass is not even dressed."

She turned to glare at him and said, "Don't you be looking at my fat ass."

Snowy was glad to see her beautiful body in the short yellowish green nightshirt and with a wolfish grin said, "Fat, I thought it was a bit lean but I guess it depends on your taste."

"Shut up and fix some coffee while I take a shower."

"Mirabel, seriously, we have to be on site for nine o'clock. Just go with your minimalist look; a little rouge and a ponytail."

Walking back into the kitchen, Mirabel stared at Snowy, "What the fuck is rouge? Listen Snowy when you start wearing a little black eye liner then you can tell me about makeup."

While Snowy made the coffee he could still feel the warmth in the room that Mirabel had radiated. He laughed to himself when he thought of the comment about the rouge and a pony tail; when he said minimalist look he was really thinking of nudity. He knew and so did Mirabel that she could wear anything and still be beautiful.

This warm shower was probably going to be the most enjoyable part of her day and so she was going to take her time and let the warm water wash away her irritation. Four years of college and numerous jobs at small local stations had led up to her dream job as a reporter for the iconic station WBTZ in the great big ass city of New York. But after six months she was tired of these fluff pieces. She was tired of being the perfect, always smiling Lois Lane. Today's assignment, a damn orchid show. Her boss, Allen Goldsky, Mr. Momma's Boy wanted someone to do a piece on the City Orchid Society which his mother was presiding chairwoman. She turned the water off to hear what Snowy was yelling. "What did you say?"

"The coffee is ready and I hope you will be soon. You don't need to get dolled up; this clip will probably air on the early morning Sunday news hour. Ten people will probably see this segment. So hurry your skinny ass up." As she dried off she knew Snowy was right, there was no need to put much effort into this assignment.

Snowy looked up and smiled when Mirabel came into the kitchen, she had taken his advice. Her minimalist look was light brown pants made of some crisp lustrous fabric, tucked into short dark brown boots and an emerald green pull-over sweater that highlighted her thick short chestnut colored hair. Very little makeup, if any and her hair pulled back into a small ponytail. Snowy thought she looked perfect. Her tough girl act couldn't hide that radiant always sexy grin; he knew that brassy sparkling wit was there to camouflage her gentle caring nature. The honey-upped voice and appealing directness in conversation had a gravitational pull on everyone that came near her orbit. "O.K., Ms. Dynamic Reporter, drink your coffee so we can get the hell out of here."

Snowy knew that they would have to stop at Silverstein's Deli for Mirabel's daily fix of a sourdough bagel with an artichoke cream cheese spread, a latte and of course her habit, her need for striking up conversations with complete strangers. Whenever Snowy teased her about her addiction to babble; her answer was always the same, "Snowy, people like to talk about themselves and everybody and I mean everybody has a story. Push the right buttons and even a hermit will paint you a picture."

At nine fifteen Snowy drove into the parking lot of the Thomas Jefferson Nondenominational Community Center or as most of the locals called it—The T J. The TJ was just a box of a building, four stories of windows and bricks. The surrounding pavilions and picnic areas was what made it popular on sunny weekends. While Snowy got his camera and gear together, Mirabel rushed to find Mrs. Goldsky. When he found Mirabel he could see Mrs. Goldsky didn't look happy and she kept jabbing her finger in the air to make some point. He could see that Mirabel had put on her look that could turn most people into stone or at least blithering idiots but had no effect on prima donnas of privilege. As Mrs. Goldsky turned to walk away Snowy could hear the patrician's voice say, "Even though you rudely missed the opening of the show, hopefully you will do a good job covering the rest of the exhibition."

Turning to face Snowy, Mirabel scrunched up her nose and said a little too loudly, "What an odious old hunchbacked troll." Snowy put his finger to his lip to signal for Mirabel to quiet down. "You know Snowy someone should tell the bitch that friends fade, but enemies accrue."

"Where would you like me to set up the camera for the first shot?"

Oh, Snowy I wish you didn't have to wear those hideous dark sunglasses. I like looking at your pink eyes. You should grow your hair longer, and then you could look like Johnny or is it Edgar Winters. One of those guys is an albino and a rock star. A rock star Snowy."

Snowy smiled and said, "Both are both."

Mirabel narrowed her eyes and said, "Is that albino-speak?"

"Mirabel they are brothers, both albino and both rock stars."

Mirabel slipped her arm around Snowy's arm, "Snowy you are the smartest white dude in all of New York City. Hmm, I think the first shot should be me introducing the show, then we can find the old hag and give her some face time, then we can just take various shots of the vagina-looking orchids. Do they look like vaginas to you; with vagina lips? What do you think Snowy?"

"I think we should shoot real soon while we still have this beautiful morning sunlight. You can stand in front of the most colorful vaginas that we can find."

"Snowy, are any of my jackets still in your car. It's a beautiful butter bright day with those great rolling puffy clouds but the air is kind of crisp."

"Sorry, no jacket, I'll look for a good spot while you get yourself ready."

The orchid show was on the East Pavilion of the TJ. There was an open field fifty or sixty yards wide separating the pavilion from the building. Trees and shrubbery with their shiny spring leaves blocked the view of the side street and also created a barrier for the morning sun. Snowy was scouting for the best light to highlight the colorful flowers and Mirabel's chestnut colored hair that sparkled hints of red in the right sunlight. "When you are ready stand in front of those baskets of flowers, we'll use them as the background." Stony pointed to hanging baskets of orchids with a riot of colors that were about shoulder-height. "If you walk, walk slowly to your right; don't turn to your left because the sun will be too fully on your face. Are you ready?" Mirabel nodded yes. "O.K., City Orchid Society, three, two, and one."

"Hi, I'm Mirabel Gaspar and on this beautiful fourth day of May I'm going to try my best to acquaint you with the city's oldest........ Whoa, what was that?" Mirabel and the Society members all turned to face the TJ. "Was that an explosion? Snowy, was that an explosion?

Listen, do you hear screaming?" Snowy was already aiming the camera at a window on the third floor of the TJ directly across from the East Pavilion. "Snowy are you getting this?" Snowy, in his action-mode ignored Mirabel's question and concentrated on getting a good shot of the woman dangling a baby out of the third floor window and screaming for help. Suddenly the woman let go of the child, he struck the ledge of the second floor window and then tumbled into the arms of a man that had miraculously appeared. Everyone at the Orchid Show let out an audible gasp and yelled 'Oh My God'. The woman in the window disappeared for a moment then reappeared dangling another child holding its arms and leaning further out the window so that the child might miss the second floor window ledge. The man that just materialized signaled for the woman to stop. He took off his shoes and started climbing the copper colored drain pipe that ran alongside the windows from the roof to the ground floor.

"Mirabel get in the picture and start some narration."

With a startled and frightened look in her eyes Mirabel took a couple of deep breaths and stepped into the picture. "We just heard an explosion and now we can hear some gunfire. The woman in the window was screaming for help and dropped a baby into the waiting arms of a man standing below the window. This volunteer savior is now climbing a drain pipe to get to the woman who is holding another baby and both are in obvious distress. The man is climbing like a monkey, no, like a caterpillar inch by inch, his legs scoot up then he reaches higher with his hands to pull his body a little further up the square shaped pipe." Mirabel looking straight into the camera said, "Everyone was just stunned motionless and this man just appeared and has taken on this task of saving lives." Stepping to the side so that Snowy could have an unhindered shot of this heroism Mirabel continued to narrate the action. "The man is now at the third floor window and he has taken the baby from the woman and tucked him close to his body. The woman is now shoving another infant towards the man and he's placing the infant next to the first. Wait, another child is coming out the window, an older child and he is now clinging to the man's back with his arms wrapped around the man's neck. The man is beginning to inch his way down; he has the two infants between his torso and the pipe and is using his arms as barriers so the infants don't come out the side. He's got a rhythm and now he is moving much faster. This man must be incredibly strong. He's down; he's down on the ground floor and placing the two infants next to the first child that had been dropped from the window. It looks like he is telling the older child to sit with the babies. Oh my God, what just happened? When the man looked up, the woman in the window had fallen or jumped and he looked up just in time to catch her head and upper body; but her legs and buttocks slammed to the ground. The people around me are saying she tried to climb down the drainpipe and slipped. Another woman is coming out of the window and the man on the ground is yelling something to her. Is he, yes he is climbing back up the pipe to rescue this woman." When the man reached the woman at the third floor window another explosion occurs and many of the fourth floor windows are blown out. Slowly the man inched down the pipe with the woman clinging to his back. When they reached the ground floor, the woman took two infants, the older child carried the third infant and the man carried the injured woman that had fallen out of the third floor window. Before the rescuer and the rescued could get to the pavilion someone started shooting at them from one of the second floor windows located closer to the front of the building. Mirabel felt a tug on her sweater, smelt an unusual smell, looking down she saw the hole in her sweater and knew she had been shot. "Oh fuck, Snowy I've been shot!" Snowy already had the camera focused on Mirabel and he could see that she had her sweater scrunched up to her neck searching her stomach for a gunshot wound. Snowy had a close up shot of Mirabel letting out a rush of air and with a look of relief put her hand through the hole in her sweater and said, "Almost." Mirabel turned toward the rescuer and the rescued, her mike towing her still leaden and trembling legs, toward the super man. She was expecting a man with a movie-ready physique and instead, disappointedly, saw a plain looking man with a slight build and deeply shaded gentle brown eyes. A small fierce smile that didn't match the emotions of his eyes was the facial feature that Mirabel would never forget. But before she could compose a question, this hero, was off running in the direction of another screaming victim. A woman, whose clothes were smoking, had come out of a first floor window and just collapsed a few feet from the building and another woman was struggling, unsuccessfully, to get out of the same window. The small unheroic-looking man ripped the woman from the window, scooped-up the still smoldering woman and with a woman under each arm ran for the shelter of the East Pavilion and the trees. Twenty feet before reaching the relative safety of the Pavilion, police who had come from the side street with rifles at their ready, rushed out to assist the hero. As the policeman reached the rescuer, gunfire exploded from a corner window on the second floor and instantly three police drop to the ground clenching gunshot wounds. The unlikely looking hero not through with his herculean efforts, grabbed a rifle from one of the fallen officers and was once again running towards danger. When the second floor gunman appeared in the window and started wildly firing in all directions, the hero dropped to one knee, raised the rifle, aimed and shot the gunman who slumped partially out of the window. The hero didn't take a second to admire his work; he was instantly again running towards the front corner of the TJ. Before he could advance more than a few yards, he dropped to his knee to aim and fire on another villain that had come around the corner of the TJ firing his weapon at the hero. The attacker scrambled back around the corner of the building; the hero stood to advance forward and then suddenly the whole front corner of the TJ crumbled and exploded outward. Mirabel screaming, "No, no, dam it no;" started racing in the direction of the hero.

Snowy following, filming and yelling, "Give me some narration."

Mirabel breathing heavy, turned to face the camera with the collapsed remains of the front corner of the TJ in the background. "This man, this man he didn't have to and he risked all. We have to put down the camera and see if we can help." When she turned to face the ruins she could see police coming out of the yellow dust floating and cloaking the remains of the building. Still mostly shrouded in the floating dust Mirabel could see two swat team members leading the hero away from the carnage. Mirabel with a look of wonder spread across her face pointed to the trio and softly said, "He's alive." Unable to contain herself, Mirabel's face twisted into a cry, "He's alive." Snowy keeping his composure, or as he liked to say, 'Being as cool as snow' had filmed everything.

"Mirabel, let's see if we can get closer to the man before they take him off for medical care. If we can get close enough, try and ask a question. What's his name or something?" Snaking their way around policeman, swat team members, firemen and EMTs they were within fifty feet of the hero when two policemen stepped in front of them and said that they were setting up crime tape and the press would have to leave the crime scene. Snowy kept his camera trained on the hero as they slowly walked him to a waiting ambulance. The hero was covered in yellow dust except where blood oozed from his wounds. He must have turned at the moment of the explosion because the left side of his shirt and pants were shredded and Snowy thought he could see teeth instead of cheek skin. Walking backwards Snowy continued to film while Mirabel made it difficult for the policemen to expel her from the crime scene. The hero suddenly stopped and cautiously turned his head as if to sample the crowd or to sniff the air, then took a few steps forward, stopped again and turned forty five degrees to his right and quickly walked searching for someone or something. The wounded man stopped in front of a thin young woman with brunette hair holding hands with an older woman. He said something to the young woman, hugged her, holding her head to his chest, turned and walked quickly to the waiting ambulance.

"Snowy don't lose that woman. Keep your eyes on her. Officers, could you guys escort us from the crime scene to the other side of the road." Both officers with wry smiles, enjoying this exchange with a beautiful woman said, "Yeah, OK, but let's move quickly." Snowy and Mirabel hustled to the other side of the road, leaving behind the two officers, keeping their focus on the two women that were walking down a side street.

"Excuse me, excuse me ladies." The older woman turned to see who was speaking but the younger woman continued staring straight ahead. When Mirabel was near she said, "I'm Mirabel Gaspar with WBTZ, the Daily News. We saw you talking to that man. He was a hero today. Do you know him?"

The older woman shading her eyes from the mid-morning sun with her free hand said suspiciously, "No, no we have no idea who he is."

"We saw him speak to your companion. Can we ask you what he said?"

The older woman turned to her companion and with both hands guided her to face Mirabel. The thin, almost frail, young woman with brown hair and pale skin was wearing dark and stylish sunglasses. Mirabel could see that the young woman's cheeks were streaked with tear stains and that the right temple area was wet and covered with dust from when the hero held her head to his chest.

With an unexpected gentleness in her voice Mirabel asked, "What did that man say to you?"

The young woman turned to fully face Mirabel said, "Did you know I was coming? Then he held me and then just quickly left." The young woman with tears again streaming down her cheeks turned to leave.

Mirabel stepping forward with mike in her hand said, "What did he mean by that? Why are you crying?"

With her back to Mirabel and in a clear high voice the young woman said, "Because I can see light." Mirabel turning to the older woman said, "I'm confused."

The older woman still holding on to the young woman with both hands knew that Mirabel was going to continue until they gave her their story. "We were returning from our daily morning walk when this horrible explosion occurred. We were just trying to get to our street so that we could get away from all of this and then suddenly this man came up and hugged Mary. She's crying because she said she can see light. She has been in total darkness for most of her life; she's been blind since she was seven years old. I told her it was just all the excitement. We're going back to the apartment, have breakfast and then rest. She'll be OK after we rest."

Mirabel could feel the fine hairs on the back of her neck moving in the nonexistent chilly breeze and the bottom of her gut was moving heavily; something was odd, she had an eerie feeling. When she recovered from her inner thoughts, Mirabel could see that the two women had continued down the side street. "What is your name?"

The older woman turned and shouted, "Vivian."

"What's your last name?"

"That's all you need to know."

"Are you her mother?"

"Yes."

"Can I call on you later?"

"Not today."

Turning to Snowy, Mirabel grabbed his arm, "Snowy watch which apartment they go into; I'm going to find out to which hospital they took our hero."

Mirabel pushed her way through the crowd, found Snowy and yelled, "St. Joseph Hospital."

Snowy, ignoring Mirabel, had his cell phone to his ear and was concentrating on the conversation, "Yes, yes, ok, ok, yes, gotcha." Putting his cell phone in his little side pouch, Snowy turned to Mirabel, "That was the station. They have a truck on site. They want us to hook up this video and they want you live. Rahm Johnson is anchoring the desk. We are going to be the first with any knowledge of what is going on and the only ones with first hand video. You are going to be big time baby. Be sure and show the bullet holes in your sweater. Pete is going to be your cameraman; I have to be in the truck."

"No Snowy, no, I need you behind the camera."

"Mirabel, Pete is a great cameraman and you can't insult him. You'll be great and as soon as you finish I'll drive you to St. Joseph."

It was now eleven P.M. and Snowy was silently driving and thinking about the day's events; Mirabel was just too tired to talk. Mirabel rolled her head left so that she could watch Snowy drive. "Snowy, please never give me fashion advice again. It was my one chance to be dolled up for the world; but instead I was wearing Mr. Snowy's minimalist couture. The new unsexy look of 2013."

Snowy laughed and said, "You were wearing the perfect look for today's participatory journalism. Don't ever throw away your bullet scarred sweater." Giggling, "And the world will never forget that look of utter terror when you thought you had been shot."

"So you think that was funny."

Breaking into a belly laugh Snowy said, "The world saw your sweater shoved under your neck so you could search your stomach for a bullet wound."

Physically drained, but her mind still racing Mirabel was already planning for the next day's events. "Snowy, you need to stay at my place tonight so that we can be on this story as soon as possible. I have some of your shirts, so you'll have some clean clothes. I don't have any clean pants for you so you'll have to wear the same ones, that is, if you didn't soil your panties when that explosion rocked us. I have cereal, milk and eggs so we can have breakfast and then go directly to St Joseph."

With a broad smile on his face Snowy thought, "Great day and now a beautiful night."

Tucked and melded into her seat Mirabel noticed Snowy's reaction and thought how handsome his profile was. "Snowy, take that damn grin off of your wolfish face and try concentrating on a plan for tomorrow. We're the rock stars of this story and we've got to keep it going, keep it hot. The hospital will be our first stop and then we have to follow up on that mother and daughter."

May 5, 6:30 a.m.

Snowy and Mirabel snuck up to the fourth floor of St. Joseph Hospital and were surprised to see so many medical staff zipping around on urgent missions. This was shift change but the night staff seemed reluctant to leave. Snowy saw a nurse that was dating one of his friends and asked her if everything was alright. The exhausted-looking nurse turned to see if any of her supervisors were around and said, "Snowy it was crazy last night. This is the floor that we put the overflow from the ICU ward. We had four that had a life expectancy range from seventy two hours to a week and then we had the Good Samaritan from yesterday's terrorist attack. Everything was pretty normal until around two this morning when we lost all power; even back up power. We were in total darkness and this was happening just on this floor. When we went to check on the patients, the doors to their rooms would not open. This shouldn't be possible, there are no locks on the doors and they are not electrically controlled. Three and four of us together could not shove those doors open. It seemed like an hour but eleven minutes later the power came back on and the doors easily opened. This is what is freaking me out. The four critical patients are walking, talking, asking for breakfast and all are showing normal vitals. And then there is the Good Samaritan; he is now in a catatonic state and his vitals are getting worse every hour. There is no plausible reason for any of this. I got to get back to work and Snowy, please don't use my name."

Mirabel knew she would need a little more information for this scoop to work. "What's his name?"

The nurse turned to leave and said over her shoulder, "The doctors and the police are just calling him The Mystery Man."

Snowy and Mirabel rushed down to the front of the hospital to shoot a segment on the information they had just received. They knew they had information that no one else had and others would probably have to wait until the mid-morning briefing that the hospital would provide and then there would be a briefing by city administrators. Mirabel was excited because she knew their report would be on air at least an hour before the other networks and they probably wouldn't have the details that they had just received. "Snowy get your camera ready. I want to write down all this info before I forget anything and before we start shooting I want you to check my notes to see if I forgot anything." Snowy's camera was always ready so he just stood there looking at Mirabel and thinking how beautiful she was in the early morning sunlight. He thought she was one of those perfect faces that didn't need to be covered up in makeup. This morning she wore just light traces of makeup and her thick hair was brushed smooth; her pastel light green A-line dress belted at the waist with a dark green scarf, which accented her hourglass figure, draped for a loose flattering fit. He didn't think her beige ankle boots were a good match with the elegant dress, but if he had mentioned it he would have been met with a smile and the same sarcastic words, "You have to buy the doll before you can dress it."

By 7:30 their segment was running on network T.V., two hours before anyone had any information on yesterday's hero. Snowy and Mirabel's next mission was to check on Vivian and Mary. Then they would rush back to catch the 10:00 scheduled briefing by city officials.

Vivian answered the door and was surprised and visibly irritated when she saw Snowy and Mirabel. Snowy knew that once she started speaking this woman like everyone else would be captured by Mirabel's charm, her savoir-vivre. Using her, I'm concerned for you, voice, Mirabel said, "Hello Vivian we're just checking on you and Mary. How is Mary doing today?"

Vivian's stern face crumbled with emotions as tears flowed she said, "We're getting ready for a doctor appointment at eleven. Mary says that she is seeing fuzzy images. It's not possible; she has been blind for most of her life. She's in a euphoric state. After the doctor appointment, she wants me to bring her to St. Joseph to see if she can see him. They just said on T.V. that he is unconscious and in critical condition."

Holding Vivian's hand Mirabel asked, "Can we talk to Mary?"

As soon as Mirabel had spoken Mary came into the room and said, "Mom whose here?"

"It's the reporters we spoke to yesterday. I'm sorry, what's your name again?"

Mirabel walked directly in front of Mary and said, "My name is Mirabel and his name is Snowy."

Mary looked directly at Mirabel, squinted her eyes and whispered, "What beautiful and unusual names."

Mirabel again in her sincere voice said, "Mary, your mother has told us that you are seeing images. Is that a result of the explosion yesterday? Did any debris hit you?"

"I see darkness and light; I can see you as a dark image on the light background. It seems like every few hours I can see just a little bit better. I am sure I was not hit by any debris from the explosion. I did feel the blast and the shocking thunder. But no debris; I did smell the dust."

"Why do you want your mother to bring you to St Joseph Hospital?" Mary's face transformed into a bright smiling image. "I want to meet my Mystery Man. I want to know what he meant when he asked me if I knew he was coming. What did he mean? I feel like I was chosen for some reason. I have seen more in the last twenty-four hours than I have seen in the last twenty years and my sight is getting stronger. My heart, my soul feels lighter, compassionate; I'm so excited. It's because of him and I need to know why."

Mirabel reached out to Mary and with an emotional tone that revealed her southern heritage asked, "Can I hold you for a minute?" Not waiting for an answer Mirabel wrapped her arms around Mary and after a long moment, pulled back and looked into Mary's eyes and claimed, "You've just given me an answer. When I saw your mystery man's face I thought I saw a look of melancholy, but now I believe it was a look of a man weighted by a mission." Hugging Mary again, Mirabel stated, "I too want to meet your Mystery Man and ask him why."

Snowy knew when Mirabel got emotional with a story she tended to lose all objectivity and if asked she would sit with this mother and daughter and drink tea and would speak about nothing for hours. "Mrs. Vivian, Miss Mary, could we include your story in our late morning report. Mirabel and I have to get back to the hospital to check on the status of the Mystery Man and to hear what the city administration says about yesterday's attack. I'm sure you need some time to get ready for your doctor's appointment."

Mrs. Vivian hesitantly expressed, "Well I don't."

Before Vivian could finish her statement Mary quickly chimed in, "Yes, yes of course. Tell everything. If people know about my situation, there will be a better chance that I will get some answers. The hospital authorities will be more likely to let me visit him. Please tell everything."

Vivian started to speak, but Snowy suddenly made a move for the door and motioning for Mirabel to follow, "Mirabel, let's get back to work and we'll see you later today or maybe tomorrow and maybe we can film a short segment." Handing Vivian a card, "This is our phone number. Maybe you can call us latter today to tell us what the doctor said." Vivian beat Snowy to the door, quickly opening it and looked relieved when Snowy and Mirabel walked out.

Walking onto the street Mirabel with a confused and aggravated look, turned to Snowy and in an irritated expression told him, "I wasn't finished."

Snowy patiently turned to her and said, "I know, but we need to get this information on the air. Sally just texted me that the station is receiving all sorts of information about our Mystery Man. She said this story is all over social media with some really wild stories."

After wading through the crowds at the hospital to hear the latest medical update on the Mystery Man and the other victims of yesterday's attack; Snowy and Mirabel then rushed to City Hall to hear the police and city administrators briefing. They filmed segments at each briefing to feed the continual hunger of the station for all news dealing with yesterday's terrorist attack. The station had two other more experienced teams with more star power covering the event; which allowed Mirabel and Snowy to freelance and get information that wasn't being mass fed to the media. They were now preparing for a live feed for the noon news hour with Rahm Johnson co-anchoring with Karen Kimball.

"Snowy, my hair looks O.K."

Snowy, occupied with trying to find the best location to film the live feed, turned to Mirabel and said, "Mirabel if we were in a hurricane your hair would look great; just relax, don't let any dead time occur because you have lots of info to give them. It's almost noon, the sun isn't directly above just yet; so I think we'll shoot from the shade of those trees across the street and have the wreckage of the TJ as the background. Let's cross the street and get into position. The news truck is here. We should start shooting in a couple of minutes."

May 5, Noon News Hour

"Welcome to the Noon News Hour, I'm Rahm Johnson and my colleague sitting next to me is Karen Kimball."

With a serious demeanor, Karen Kimball looked directly into the camera and stated, "We want to give you the latest on yesterday's terrorist attack; we have Blaine Breaux with coverage at St. Joseph Hospital and Steve Redmire with coverage at City Hall, but first we'll start with Mirabel Gaspar at the TJ, the scene of yesterday's carnage. Mirabel what do you have for us?"

A slight breeze was gently blowing Mirabel's hair away from her face and the soft light made the tragic scene almost intimate. Looking through the camera Snowy thought Mirabel looked stunning; he knew he could not have positioned her for a better shot. "Hello Karen, the hospital confirmed our earlier report that the Mystery Man, yes that's what everyone is calling him, is in a catatonic state, not quite a coma and his vitals are poor. He is still in intensive care in critical condition. They are not sure why the catatonic state, there are no physical reasons for this condition. City Hall is confirming that the attackers were both foreign and home grown terrorists. They believe all the attackers were killed yesterday; but their investigation is looking for others that may have had connections with these terrorists. They aren't saying much because the investigation is still in its very early stage. They are looking at a lot of video, including ours, for any clues. They think they know the identity of the Mystery Man, but are holding that information until further into the investigation and also to protect him from any retaliation from this terrorist group. This story is all over the social media and."

Rahm cut off Mirabel in mid-sentence, "Stay with us Mirabel. We're going to cut away to Steve Redmire who is providing coverage at City Hall."

Now that she was off camera Mirabel let out a rush of air and then took in a giant breath. "Snowy, do I look nervous?"

"Mirabel you look like you should be anchoring an evening news show. You look beautiful; you're doing a great job. Relax and don't be afraid to tell Rahm to wait a minute, he has a tendency to get bits and pieces from a variety of sources. O.K., you ready, they're coming back to you."

"Yes, Karen as I was saying, social media is going wild with stories about the Mystery Man. But before I get to that, we've been following a related story. Yesterday after the explosion we saw the Mystery Man, I like to call him the Hero, wrap his arms around a young woman and hug her before getting into the ambulance. Well that young woman also does not know who the Mystery Man is, but she is a woman that has been blind for over twenty years and now can see images. We talked to her and her mother this morning and they had a doctor's appointment to see what was happening. She reported to me that her vision is improving every hour."

Karen Kimball shot back, "That's incredible. That's like Jesus healing the sick. What did the doctor say?"

Mirabel knew she would only have seconds to say everything that she had in her report so she started to rush her speech. "Karen, this story plus what happened at the hospital last night is so mysterious, supernatural, I mean really spine chilling. This young woman's doctor's appointment is this afternoon and of course we will be talking to her. Karen, probably the number one story on social media dealing with our Hero is the 2011 plane crash in British Columbia."

"Mirabel stay with us we have to cut away for a station break and then Blaine Breaux has some news for us from St. Joseph Hospital." Rahm Johnson turned to Karen and said, "This all just so incredible."

"Snowy, is the plane crash video ready to roll? How am I doing?"

"You're doing great. Rahm wants us to stick to just yesterday's events. He said we'll deal with related stories later."

Mirabel's soft facial features hardened and her chin rose in defiance. "Snowy, fuck Rahm and his plastic face; this plane crash story is related news. It's the news buzzing all over social media."

Snowy smiled, he loved to see Mirabel when she felt offended and was ready to take on the world. He also knew that she held Rahm in contempt because of an Eskimo and albino joke that he thought was hilarious. "Mirabel, don't accidently let an F bomb slip or you'll be working on a one page newspaper in Nowhere, Louisiana. We'll stick to our script and see where that takes us. Just don't get competitive with Rahm on air. His ego is very fragile; so remember don't confront him."

"Fahcrissake Snowy, don't lecture me. Am I talking too fast?"

"Mirabel you are a pro. You're doing great. We're losing the shade. Come in about five feet. O.K. the station break is over; Blaine is just about finished so get ready."

"Karen, as I was saying before the break there are stories flying around social media and the most intriguing one is the plane crash in Canada two years ago."

In his deep baritone voice Rahm said, "That's all intriguing but is there any new information about the terrorist attack?"

In a voice a little too steely, "Rahm, if you let me finish you'll see that this is a very important part of yesterday, today and tomorrow's events. In February of 2011, a plane carrying twelve passengers and crew crashed into the Skeena River in British Columbia. A man repeatly dove into the freezing river and rescued nine of the passengers. Bystanders filmed this Good Samaritan as he pulled survivors out of the freezing water. After he rescued the last survivor he pulled himself out of the freezing river and walked away. No one knows the name of this anonymous hero. People are saying this man and yesterday's hero are one in the same. We are going to roll some video and let you see the resemblance." As the TV viewers saw the video of the Canadian rescue, Mirabel gave a running commentary. "As you can see the Good Samaritan had dark hair and a slight build just like yesterday's hero; but look at those eyes and that mouth. They both have that look of having a burden they must endure."

Rahm could be heard clearing his voice, "Interesting, interesting."

"There are hundreds of different stories about our hero. This will be real quick. We spoke to a Nancy Miller from St. Louis. She said that our hero was her neighbor for two years and his name was Angel Mathias. When she and her husband divorced they let Mr. Mathias decide who would get their dog. On the day he was to decide he told her and her ex-husband that he had the dog put to sleep. She cried, her ex-husband didn't seem to care. It was just a test. He wanted to see who had the most love for the dog. He awarded her the dog."

Karen hurriedly interrupted Mirabel, "A Solomonic decision; a hero, a good Samaritan and a man as wise as Solomon. This woman said his name was Angel Mathias and she's sure her Solomon and yesterday's hero are the same?"

"Yes."

Before Mirabel could add to her answer Karen quickly said, "Thank you Mirabel, we'll be taking a station break and when we come back we will report on the world's reaction to this latest terrorist attack."

May 5, 11:00 PM

Snowy and Mirabel sat at her small cluttered kitchen table, both in a daze, eating cold breakfast cereal. Raising her drawn, fatigued face Mirabel said, "Hey, did you call your neighbor to feed Lucy? How old is that old mutt?"

Too tired for conversation Snowy answered in a weary, monotone voice. "Yes. Twelve."

"Do you think I made Rahm angry?"

Still staring at his bowl of cold cereal Snowy managed a weak smile. "After lecturing him and twice correcting him on air, he is probably at this moment pacing in his bedroom plotting your destruction."

"We've been at it for forty eight hours; we have to slow down tomorrow. After we sleep for eight hours, we'll scoot by your apartment to get you some clothes and then a huge breakfast: eggs, bacon, pancakes and two lattes."

Before Mirabel could continue her breakfast dream Snowy perked up, "Mirabel you're the star of this story, we can rest when this story dies out. We'll have a whole team working with us tomorrow. Eleanor will be with us tomorrow to help with your hair and to give you some pointers. In a week this story will already be back page news and if you don't keep doing your best you'll once again be doing orchid shows."

In an exhausted whisper, "Orchid shows aren't so bad."

They looked into each other's eyes and tried unsuccessfully to hold back the giggles. "Thank you Snowy. Thank you so much for getting the perfect shots. Thank you for making my job so much easier. I just can't imagine working with anyone else."

Mirabel knew that Snowy had an open job offer to work for the International News Agency. He wasn't just a great cameraman; he knew the business. He would be based in Rome. The countries surrounding the Mediterranean Sea would be his news beat. He wouldn't be just behind the camera. He had the opportunity to do documentaries and feature stories on the chaos that was engulfing that region. She wasn't sure why he hadn't yet taken the job; she hoped it was because of her.

Drunk with exhaustion, her social shield down, she asked, "Do you think we make a good team? Not just in journalism, but you know, you know what I mean."

Snowy was now fully alert, his emotions wrecked by exhaustion look directly into Mirabel's eyes. "We make a great team. When I'm with you I can feel the air surrounding us pop and sizzle like it's electrically charged. I feel like a champion. I feel like I'm on the best team, the right team."

May 6, Monday Morning, 9:00 AM

Mirabel was glad that she had brought her teal green blazer, she had been expecting a cool morning, but it turned out to be unusually crisp for early May. It wasn't the temperature but the sky that had everyone's attention. The morning sunlight had a faded vermillion tinge similar to an evening sunset, and the puffy white and gray clouds were edged on their eastern side in indigo and lavender. The clouds were moving from the northwest to the southeast at a rapid pace, like they had a specific mission. The billowy gray clouds had a 3D effect that made their darker centers appear closer than they really were.

Mirabel and Snowy thought they would sneak into the hospital, like yesterday morning, but it was impossible because of the crowds of people surrounding the huge hospital that encompassed most of a city block. Security was tight, abundant and aggressively checking the identification of all who attempted to enter the hospital. Media was allowed only in a designated area. The huge crowd was in a festive mood. There were people singing; others were chanting; some were praying. There were the flag wavers and the T-shirt sellers. If the people in the crowd weren't talking about the morning sky, then they were talking about the Good Samaritan, the Hero, the Mystery Man. Some were even pointing to the unusual morning sky and saying that it was a sign, staring upward as if waiting for Michelangelo's hand of God to appear.

Mirabel didn't mind being the center of attention, but she wasn't prepared to be recognized by so many in the crowd. People in the crowd would stop what they were doing when they saw her and stare. She now had an army to do the work that she and Snowy once did as a team of two. She had junior reporters searching the crowd for interesting people so she could have someone to interview. She had an assistant to help her rewrite her notes into clear, to the point, reports. She had an extra cameraman. She had a hair and makeup assistant and of course Eleanor was there to coordinate everything. Eleanor, dressed in a sleek and stylish turquoise blue pencil skirt and tan cashmere light sweater, tried to convince her to wear a Clintonian pantsuit that she had brought to the apartment early that morning. Mirabel refused the pantsuit and opted for her crepe de chine royal blue dress. The dress that Snowy liked because he said the color made her brown eyes stand out and hypnotize. After the hospital's daily morning briefing Mirabel was ready to go on air for the first of many reports.

Eleanor checking out Mirabel's makeup and hair with a critical eye, smiled and said, "You look great. Try not being so confrontational with Rahm. Work with him and he'll make you shine. Mr. Goldsky called; he wants you to call him when you get a break."

In a defensive tone, Mirabel inquired, "What does he want? Is there a problem?"

With her motherly smile and thin hair dancing in the breeze Eleanor replied, "I don't think there is a problem yet, just mind your manners."

"Oh fuck him and Rahm with his Napoleonic Complex."

Eleanor's motherly smile turned into an angry stare, "Mirabel you represent many people so be professional. You had better learn to curb that salty tongue of yours. Everyone is ready. Rahm will be cutting to you in a few seconds."

Mirabel with a smile, her smile, which made goofy boys out of men, was ready for the world. "Good morning Rahm. The hospital spokesman has just finished his daily morning report. Some of the victims of the terrorist attack, after receiving treatment at other facilities were then transferred to St. Joseph. All of these patients have been released. The only victim of the terrorist attack that is still being treated at this facility is the man without a name. People are calling him an American Hero and a Good Samaritan. Bruce Guillot, the hospital spokesman, said this patient has been upgraded from critical to stable and that he is slowly coming out of the catatonic state. He stated that there is still no explanation for this patient going into this comatose state.

Rahm in his deep baritone voice and with a hint of humor broke in, "We could also add the name Solomon. Mirabel, what of those patients in the same ward, on their death beds, who inexplicably were cured. It's like a miracle."

Calmly Mirabel agreed. "Yes, yes Rahm. It's like a miracle. The hospital spokesperson said that these four patients are doing remarkably well and once again there is no medical explanation."

Determined to show that he was not angry over yesterday's exchanges Rahm, a bit too cheerfully, announced, "Mirabel Gaspar, our star reporter, has become as much of the news as our American Hero. Mirabel, you've been with this story from the beginning. You were one of the few eyewitnesses to the whole event. Can you give us a sense of what it's been like to be covering such a fascinating and sometimes bizarre story? Do you have an update on the miraculous story, the stunning story of the young blind woman? Who are all those people milling about? It looks like there are thousands of people crowding the parking lots and the streets. What are they waiting for?"

And the fight was on. Mirabel looking straight into the camera gave her best; 'Don't patronize me' stare. "Rahm, that's quite a few questions. But first you used the word bizarre. That's too common, too ordinary. I'd rather call it magical, maybe mystical, celestial, of course quixotic and definitely heroic. The blind girl you referred to is Mary. She has requested that we withhold, for now, her last name. We will interview her by phone this afternoon. She has another doctor's appointment today and we will speak to her after the doctor visit. She said that by the end of the week she'd like us to film an interview. As far as the crowd, we've talked to police that estimate the crowd at fifteen to twenty thousand. Whatever the number; this crowd has stopped all traffic in this section of the city. You can see people are still streaming in from the side streets. In some sense, it's a circus atmosphere, but mostly people seem to be waiting for a larger event. I talked to one man and he said he just wanted to see the hero with his own eyes. Rahm, I have with me Mr. Simon Betters."

In his best 'Voice of God' impersonation, Rahm broke in, "Mirabel hold on to Mr. Betters. We have to take a station break and when we get back we'll hear what he has to say."

Eleanor rushed to Mirabel to reposition her. She wanted her facing into the wind so that her hair would not blow into her face and Snowy wanted the soft morning sunshine directly on her face. Mirabel gripped Mr. Betters hand and dragged him to her new position.

Mr. Betters looked on in intrigue as Eleanor moved in close to Mirabel and said, "Everyone likes it when you spar with Rahm, but don't be mean, unpleasant, simple and definitely don't be stupidly vulgar. Smile, use your haughty wit." Her finger pointed at Mirabel, Eleanor gave her best sparkling smile, "Haughty wit, not castrating wit. The break should be over by now. Get ready. Don't stare into the camera Mr. Betters." Eleanor walked back to the team and Mirabel stood there gripping Mr. Betters arm waiting for her opponent.

Rahm's deep baritone voice came booming loudly into Mirabel's earpiece, "Our correspondent, Mirabel Gaspar, is at St. Joseph Hospital, covering the continuing bizarre story of this mystery man, the hero from yesterday's terrorist attack. Mirabel you have something for us?"

Still gripping Mr. Betters's arm, Mirabel put her killer smile into gear. "Rahm, when you hear this story you gonna want to come up with a better word than bizarre. Bizarre is a little too easy and overused. Mr. Simon Betters is a teacher at Robert E. Lee Elementary School in Churchville, Tennessee. Rahm, if you recall this was the scene of a school shooting about two and a half years ago. Let me give Mr. Betters this opportunity to tell his story."

With the soft bustle of conversation in the background, Mr. Betters stood woodenly and spoke softly to Mirabel, "This man you call, The Hero, is Mr. Peter Nazreth. He was our school guidance counselor. When the gunman started shooting, everyone ran from the gun shots; Mr. Nazreth was seen running towards the direction of the gun shots. The gunman entered a second grade class and had leveled his gun at the teacher. Before he could pull the trigger, the gunman was attacked and killed. Every student said that it was a tiger that attacked the gunman and then it was Mr. Nazreth that got off the dead gunman. The teacher said she closed her eyes and waited for the bullet, then heard a loud thud, opened her eyes and saw Mr. Nazreth guiding her students out of the room. He resigned his position two weeks later and we've never seen him again."

Mirabel leaned forward to be closer to Mr. Betters and slowly said, "Mr. Betters are you sure that this Mr. Peter Nazreth and our Mystery Man is the same person."

Mr. Betters turned to stare at the camera and stated sincerely, "Mr. Nazreth and the hero in that hospital is definitely the same person. They have the exact slight wiry build, the brown hair, and the heavy eyes, eyes that seemed to be carrying a heavy burden. Then the small fierce smile that sometimes looked like a teasing sneer."

"Why did you come here? Did you drive up from Tennessee?"

Turning to face Mirabel, Mr. Betters's solemn expression held his emotions in check and explained, "When I saw his face on the television, I knew I had to see this man one more time. Forty people from our community drove nonstop from Tennessee. We all have the same desire to speak to Peter one more time and to thank him for showing such courage."

"Thank you Mr. Betters and I hope you and your friends get to speak to this uncommon man. As do I, it would be a privilege to spend time with this man." Turning to the camera, Mirabel had a serious expression on her face, "Rahm don't call this story bizarre, call it heroic. I have Sean Haley from Silver Beach, Maine that has an interesting story for us."

"We have to go to a station break," Rahm announced in a clearly irritated voice, "We will be right."

Not waiting for Rahm to finish his statement Mirabel said, "Rahm this will only take a second. Four years ago Mr. Haley had been laid off from his job that he had held for fifteen years, he lost his medical insurance, his wife was in a serious car accident that brought huge medical expenses and his daughter had just started college. He didn't know where to turn. He couldn't pay his bills and his family was on the verge of losing their house. Mr. Healy, quickly explain what happened next."

A deep lyrical voice came out of the giant standing next to Mirabel. "One bright Sunday morning, we'd just come back from church and our neighbor that lived next door for about a year had packed all of his belongings into a rental truck. When we went over to ask what he was doing. He just said that it was time to move on and see new places. Then he gave us a check for eighteen thousand dollars and said he hoped it would help us through our tough times and that he could see a bright future for our family. We were suspicious, but the check cleared and we are doing great."

"Quickly Mr. Healy, what was your neighbor's name and why are you here today?"

Mr. Healy turned to the camera and said, "His name was Paul Galeo and he is the hero that everyone wants to see. My family just wants to hold him, hug again once again. We had never really showed him love, any compassion; he was just our neighbor."

Snowy walked with the camera to his right so that when Mirabel turned to face the camera the late morning, but still soft, sunshine would once again shine on her face. The partly cloudy vermillion sky had slowly turned into an enameled celestial blue sky with light amber golden sunshine. "I could give you remarkable stories like that all day. So many of these people have a story about our hero; many people made the pilgrimage just to be near such a dynamic man. Back to you Rahm."

Mirabel smiled as she heard in her earpiece Rahm's normally steady cadence, now rushed and maybe a pitch higher. "Thank you for that piece Mirabel; we'll be taking a station break and when we come back we'll bring you, our audience, some of today's other news stories."

Mirabel huddled with her team and accepted a cup of coffee that was handed to her. She turned to face Snowy, smiled and raised her cup of coffee. "Coffee, we must be big time, want some?"

Eleanor broke into the huddle, beamed her motherly smile and said, "Mr. Goldsky called. He likes how you are putting heat on Rahm. Be careful, don't go overboard. Keep it subtle. Rahm called and he's pissed. He said to remind you that he is the anchor and that he and the news director are the conductors of the news hour and for you not to forget it."

Snowy watched as Mirabel stood there, Queen for the Day, as her worker bees fluttered around tending to her every need, but he could see that her thoughts were far away. There was concern framing her face.

After a number of mid-morning on-air reports and a few more interviews, it was evident that every time Rahm acknowledged Mirabel, his words were dripping with contempt, his remarks were critical and sarcastic. Mirabel regally did her job, stayed composed and serene. She knew Rahm was looking like an ass and would never recover from this day. For a long time she had wanted to punch Rahm on the nose, but he was providing the knockout for her. By early afternoon they had mined enough stories from the hospital crowd. Garnett Hills, the beauty that the station had been grooming to possibly be a co-anchor with Rahm was assigned to St. Joseph Hospital and Mirabel and her crew were sent uptown to the Police Central Command. NYPD had new information on the terrorist attack and there was going to be a statement dealing with the American hero. Before going uptown they could swing by Mary's apartment to see how her sight was improving so that they could include her update on the five o'clock news.

When the worker bees eventually stopped circling their Queen, Snowy sat next to Mirabel and asked her what was wrong. "Snowy, I don't like all this silliness. I much rather when it was just you and I taking our time and enjoying each boring assignment. I don't like these people. Rahm is a pretentious ass who thinks he's a superstar. Last week we would have been lucky if Eleanor had given us a little nod of her head. She even said that I don't pronounce the correctly. I felt like shoving a th down her throat. I thought this is what I wanted and now I'm confused because I'm not sure. By the way, you have to stay at my place tonight."

Smiling, but keeping a professional distance, Snowy said, "You're just exhausted. You've worked too many hours. This is all new for you. There have been huge changes to your routine. But you are doing a great job and know this, in two weeks, when everything slows down, you will be wishing for some of this excitement."

Suddenly Eleanor broke through the crowd and with flailing arms summoned the entourage. "The police chief will be giving his statement in about five minutes. Billy I want you to film the whole news conference. Snowy, you concentrate on Mirabel. Mirabel, let's get closer so you can ask questions."

The news conference lasted forty five minutes and ended in time for it to be the lead story on the evening news. The worker bees were now getting their Queen ready for the big show. Snowy moved Mirabel out of the crowd and away from the early evening shadows. He found a spot where the dying sun's rays had just enough power to illuminate Mirabel and the background sign that read New York Metropolitan Police. Mirabel could hear Rahm's deep Ted Knight voice in her earpiece saying, "Good evening ladies and gentleman. We have breaking news concerning the terrorist attack. We are going to take you to the Police Central Command where a news conference has just ended. Our correspondent, Mirabel Gaspar has the latest. Mirabel what news do you have for us?"

Staring straight into the camera, Mirabel's usual look of assurance and composure was now replaced with an expression of angst and uneasiness. "Rahm, the news conference ended just a few minutes ago.

Chief Aaron Hebert said they know who some of the terrorist were. He spoke about it being a union of international and homegrown terrorist. Rahm, we're now going to show you some of that news conference."

As soon as the news conference started airing the worker bees swarmed on Mirabel, straighting loose hairs and powdering any shiny areas.

"Rahm, the Chief said that, so far, no terrorist organization is taking credit for the attack. It's still early in the investigation and they will have more info at a briefing tomorrow morning. Also with every feel good story there are always a few dark areas or dark corners in a person's life. Our American hero, the Good Samaritan, the Mystery Man or as you have called him, Solomon, has had a few scrapes with the law. The police are still not releasing his name, but he was fingerprinted in the hospital and from fingerprint identification we know a little more about this man. Three weeks ago outside of Elohim City, Arkansas he was arrested for driving his car one hundred five miles an hour in a sixty five speed zone. Marijuana was found in his vehicle, but he was not charged with driving under the influence. Seven weeks ago in Chicago he was involved in an altercation at a movie theater. It seems some seventeen year old boys cut the line. When they were confronted by other patrons waiting in line the teens started beating the patrons. Our Mystery Man got involved and when it was all over one of the teens had a broken arm and seventeen facial stiches. The other teen had a dislocated shoulder. It turns out the teenagers were African American and they accused our Mystery Man of calling them the N word. The other patrons said that did not happen. He was taken in for questioning but no charges were filed. And one other thing quickly, in January of this year in Las Vegas outside of a grocery store, a woman by the name of Bunny Smith accused him of taking her parking spot. Witnesses said that she cursed him and then spit on his face. He turned to walk back to his vehicle and the woman jumped on his back and started punching on the back of his head. He subsequently reached over and grabbed her by the hair and flipped her over his back onto the parking lot pavement. She suffered a broken leg in two places and a fracture hip joint. Again the police took him in for questioning but because of the witnesses he was not charged with any crime.

Ms. Smith's lawyers have been trying to locate the Mystery Man because they want to file a civil suit. Rahm, back to you."

In a gentle thoughtful tone Rahm asked, "Who is this man? Yes, he has the wisdom of Solomon, but he seems to be in search of something like Captain Ahab. What is his White Whale? He has crisscrossed this nation and has had some impact wherever he has roamed. When we come back we'll have the latest on the miraculous story of Mary, the once blind young woman."

The worker bees and their master, Eleanor, surrounded the Queen. Eleanor handed Mirabel a cup of water, smiled and said, "You and Rahm make a good team when both of you are civil to each other. Let's finish the day on a high. You don't have to wave a white flag of surrender. Use that man-killer charm that you have in abundance. They are almost ready for you."

For the fiftieth time today Mirabel could hear Rahm's booming voice in her ear piece. "We've all heard the story of Mary a young woman that had been blind for most of her life and then she was touched by our Hero and like a miracle she began to see light. Our correspondent, Mirabel Gaspar, has had an exclusive relationship with this young woman. Mirabel, what's the latest on this miraculous story?"

"Rahm, it's all good news. We met with Mary this afternoon and she is reporting that she has twenty- twenty vision in her right eye and her left eye is still a little blurry but improving every day. We spoke by phone with her doctor, Dr. Richard, and he has no explanation other than a miracle. Mary and her mother have agreed to meet next week with Dr. Richard, some of his colleagues and a few national known ophthalmologists to try and find an answer. I'm Mirabel Gaspar, reporting from the uptown Police Central Command. Rahm, I enjoyed working with you today."

On everyone's TV was a picture of Rahm beaming from ear to ear, "Likewise."

Mirabel heated a frozen pizza in the oven while Snowy opened a bottle of wine. "When I went to see Mr. Goldsky he had nothing but praise. He kept saying that our ratings were through the roof. I couldn't help picturing me giving him a karate chop to the neck and then riding his fat back and twisting his ear saying, "If my little piggy doesn't squeal I gonna rip your ear off." Did you know that last week he fired old Bill Hennessey? They refused to grant him a two month leave for health reasons; so he took the two months anyway. Goldsky fired him. Bill worked for the station for twenty-seven years never with more than two weeks' vacation. That's when people come back to work with a gun. He also told me that Vanity Fair had called and asked if I'd call a Brenda Vicario. Turns out Mr. Snowy Man they want to do a photo shoot. I told them sure; I'd love to do a photo shoot. But there would have to be two conditions. First condition, I want to be photographed with a handsome man and second condition, under no circumstances would there be any sunglasses. I want the world to see your beautiful pink eyes."

Pouring a glass of wine, then handing it to Mirabel and with a serious expression Snowy said, "And did you ask this handsome man if it was OK with him."

Smiling, she leaned in and kissed him on the cheek, "Oh you will or I will kick your cute little ivory white ass. I need a favor. After I shower could you give me a foot massage? My feet are killing me."

Sitting on the couch with his glass of wine Snowy said, "Yes, and the photo shoot, are they going to title it, Beauty and the Beast?"

Snuggling up to Snowy, Mirabel put her face in his neck and whispered, "I already told them that they had to name it Lucky Girl gets her Prince."

Sniffing the air Snowy said, "I guess the Prince better learn to cook cause the Lucky Girl is burning a frozen pizza."

Mirabel jumped off the couch and pulled the sizzling pizza out of the oven. "Snowy, I've also decided that once this story starts to become old news I'm going sit and think about other options. I know just reporting what is given to me is not what I want to do. I want to be in journalism, but I want to create something that informs the masses. Investigative journalism, I don't know, I just feel confused, unsatisfied and a little angry. Maybe another network with people I like. "

May 7, 6:00 A.M.

"Oh crap, its six o'clock, Mirabel you didn't set the alarm. We're supposed to be at the station for six," Snowy jumped out of bed frantically searching for his clothes, "Damn. Get your butt out of bed."

Mirabel pulled the covers over her head and said something that Snowy could not hear.

Snowy crawling on the floor looking for his shoes yelled, "What did you say?"

Mirabel peaked out from under the covers and in a croaky voice said, "Don't start the day yelling at me. Did you know that your snow-white ass glows in the dark?"

Ignoring her comments Snowy went into the kitchen and yelled, "I'll fix some coffee and toast. Hurry and get dressed. I'll call the station and tell them we'll be about an hour late."

Before the coffee was made Mirabel walked into the kitchen wearing a black knit blazer jacket, its four buttons fastened exposing only her white shirt's spread collar. Her black knit riding pants were tucked into dark brown riding boots. Her hair wasn't combed and her face didn't have any makeup. "Just give me a cup of coffee. I'll let my assistants get me breakfast and fix my face. I'm ready."

The sight of Mirabel calmed Snowy. He thought to himself that she looked so beautiful, even right out of bed. She could wear anything, mud covered overalls, a garbage bag, anything and she'd still be enchantingly beautiful.

Everyone was quiet as Snowy drove the network van to their first destination, St. Joseph's Hospital. Mirabel sat on the back bench seat, staring straight ahead as her assistants; one on each side worked on her hair and applied makeup to her expressionless face. Mirabel was angry and frustrated with herself. She was having an opportunity to further her career, to maybe even be a major player for one of the networks. In just a couple of days she had become a celebrity. People could follow the story on any network, but they were watching WTBZ to see her and her coverage of the story. The network's ratings had never been as high as the last week's ratings. Yet it all felt wrong.

She was realizing that she wasn't interested in being the pretty face in front of the camera. But this is what she had trained for since she was in high school. She wished it was just she and Snowy in the van so that she could talk to him and express her feelings. She always felt better after expressing her emotions and thoughts to Snowy. He saw life, the world, as it was; he made it easier for Mirabel to weigh the good against the bad. He wasn't just her best friend, her lover; he was everything she needed, everything she had been looking for.

Snowy's strong, clear, confident voice broke the silence, "It's remarkable the drastic change in the weather. Yesterday was cool with a soft light and the sky was odd but a wonder. Today the sky is one huge cloud. It's like a puffy, gray, velvety fog has pushed aside the sunshine. The air is heavy and moist. It looks like vampire weather. I think we all overdressed for this thick heat. Did anyone listen to the weather report this morning?"

Mirabel's petite assistant said in her perfect Queen's English, "Last night the Weather Girl said we should have a repeat of yesterday's weather. So maybe this shall pass."

Snowy pulled into the parking area reserved for the media. They were late, very late. Some of the media were already leaving. The medical briefing from the hospital administration must already be over. The crowds looked thinner, but there seemed to be some people marching and yelling in front and on the left corner of the hospital. Snowy squeezed the van into a parking spot, turned off the engine and told everyone, "O.K. guys lets go to work." As Snowy stepped from the van he could see Eleanor approaching with a mask of irritation, wearing a light blue raincoat belted at the waist and sporting a high bouncy ponytail.

Eleanor's eagle-eyed stare fixed on Mirabel as soon as she stepped out of the van. "I hope high ratings have not already gone to your head. You don't oversleep and hurt the team."

Mirabel's face did not portray any emotions. "Sorry Boss, where do we start?"

Eleanor handed Mirabel a clipboard. "I took down notes from the hospital briefing. You can go over what I have. We'll start with you rehashing the briefing or you can just strictly read the notes since you don't seem yet awake. Then you can question some of the protesters to see what their complaint is."

Mirabel's veil of uninterest disappeared when she heard the word protesters. "Protesters! What the hell can the idiots be protesting?"

Eleanor keeping her inquisitive gaze on Mirabel's face said, "That's what we want you to find out dear." Turning to Snowy, Eleanor spoke to him as an equal, she knew he was the best cameraman that they had and that he could find a job with any network. She suspected he was still at WBTZ because of Mirabel. "Snowy you don't have to worry about lighting today. So try to get her where you can see the protesters in the background and then follow her as she walks over to interview them. One interview then we'll cut back to Rahm, so that we can dry her off, this mist seems to be getting a little heavier."

Mirabel unbuttoning her jacket with one hand and fanning herself with her other hand said, "My God this heat is stifling."

Eleanor's motherly smile was back, "You definitely wore the wrong clothes for today's weather. We'll put you in the van with the air condition on high after each segment. We won't be here long because the police commissioner is giving an update on the terrorist attack at eleven. You'll be O.K. Let's get started. Snowy set her up and let us know when you are ready so that we can alert the station."

As they were walking towards the front of the hospital Snowy felt a need to give Mirabel some encouragement. "On camera you always look hot, so today won't be any different. I'll make sure you don't melt the camera."

Mirabel smiled and looked up at Snowy and said, "I know you will take care of me."

"O.K. stand here and then after you give the few lines on the hospital briefing, I'll pan over to the protesters as you walk over to do the interview. They've already spoken to Mohammed Jefferson that has agreed to speak to you for their group. Are you ready?" Mirabel shook her head yes and Snowy turned to signal Eleanor that they were ready.

Mirabel could hear in her earpiece the now familiar voice which always stoked an emotion that she usually could control – rage. Rahm in his perfectly pitched baritone voice was introducing Mirabel. "We have our correspondent Mirabel Gaspar at St. Joseph Hospital to give us the latest on the victims of the terrorist attack. What news do you have for us at this hour?"

Mirabel knew that last statement was Rahm's way of noting her late start. "Good Morning Rahm. The hospital briefing has just finished and we have all good news. The hospital spokesman, Bruce Guillot, said that all victims of the terrorist attack are doing fine and have been released from the hospital. The four miracle patients that were sharing the hospital floor with our Hero are all doing incredible. In fact, two of the patients have been allowed to return home and if the other two continue their rapid and miraculous improvement, they too will soon be going home. To continue with the good news, our Hero, our American Hero, is completely out of the coma, moving around and eating. The doctors are saying that if he continues his rapid improvement that in about a week he could be released from the hospital."

Rahm's hated voice was again in her earpiece. "That is good news. In fact, that is wonderful news. Mirabel, who are those people behind you marching and carrying signs; are they protesters of some sort?"

Mirabel turned to face the protesters and said, "'Yes they are protesting something. We have a Mohammed Jefferson that has agreed to talk to us." As she walked towards the two dozen protesters she could see some of the signs they were carrying. One sign said "Stop Black Genocide" another read "Protect our Black Sons". "Mr. Jefferson, thanks for speaking with us. What exactly are you protesting?"

Mr. Jefferson's shirt seemed to be struggling to keep his enormous stomach corralled. The thickening heat left huge patches of wet on his shirt and shorts. Mirabel could relate because she could feel the perspiration trickling down her back and her damp hair was beginning to stick to her face. "We are here to protest the continuing attacks on our black children. This man brutally attacked two teenagers and he was never charged with a crime. This has to stop. Our black children are being killed in unprecedented numbers and people are just walking free."

Mirabel heard enough, "Mr. Jefferson, did you hear the whole report? Did you not hear that the two young men were attacking people that were in line for the theatre and this hero that you are protesting tried to stop them from harming others?"

Sweat was dribbling off of Mr. Jefferson's chin when he angrily pointed a finger at Mirabel and blurted, "There are other ways to defuse a situation without breaking the bones of children."

"So you just took off of work, drew up some posters and came here to protest a man that in most people's eyes is an American hero. Do you have a job?" Mirabel was ready for a fight. "Did you see?"

Before Mirabel could finish her attack Mr. Jefferson yelled, "What the hell does me having a job have to do with Black Genocide? This is another case of the media taking sides and blaming the victims."

Calmly Mirabel stared straight into Mr. Jefferson's eyes and said, "Thank you for your comments Mr. Jefferson. This man that you are protesting has saved many lives. His heroics are on film for all to see." As Mr. Jefferson started to respond Mirabel turned away from him and said, "Back to you Rahm."

Rahm in his calm response, "You were kind of hard on Mr. Jefferson, don't you think Mirabel? This is America. We all have the right to protest anything."

Snowy could see that Mirabel was ready for a fight. He just hoped that she would not turn the air blue with her penchant for cursing.

"No Rahm I was not hard on Mr. Jefferson and yes he can protest till the dead rise up for all I care. I am not going to let these people who always have to stand up and proclaim themselves the victims to tarnish the heroic deeds of this man that is now in a hospital because he took action to help people. One has duties to our society that exceeds merely existing in it. This man took action and saved people's lives. He wasn't sitting behind a desk looking into the lens of a camera. He was volunteering his life to save others."

"O.K., O.K. I hear you." Rahm wanted to end this conversation quickly. "Mirabel thanks for that report. We will be taking a station break. Go dry off." Rahm was relieved that the words slamming around in his brain didn't come out. Why did this girl always make him teeter on losing his composure?

Mirabel's assistants each grasped an arm and escorted her to the waiting air conditioned van. Mirabel felt a sense of relief when the van's cold air hit her. She fell into her seat and mumbled to herself, "I don't feel like dealing with Rahm or any other idiots." The assistants closed the van's curtains and stripped Mirabel of her jacket and shirt. They started to help her into a navy blue sleeveless satin shirt when she stopped them and said, "My bra is soaked. I got to take it off. I'm just gonna go braless."

Both assistants quickly blurted out, "No way, Eleanor would kill us if you went on camera without a bra. We've got you another shirt; we'll try to get you another bra before we get to the police commissioner's briefing. Put this shirt on so we can start working on your hair and makeup."

Mirabel closed her eyes as her assistants worked on her face and hair. She mumbled to herself, "It's such a hideously hot day. It feels sinister out there. Even the mist is warm. I can feel water in my boots."

Eleanor stuck her head into the van and said, "O.K. ladies, are we about ready? Mirabel there is a small group of women protesting. I want you to interview one of them. A Simone St. Federica has agreed to talk to you. Once we finish with her, we'll head to the police commissioner's briefing. Look, it's too early to be fighting with Rahm. Calm down. Let's go."

When Mirabel walked up to the group of women protesters she could see that they were carrying signs that read American Hero that had a big red cross through it and written below was American Misogynist. She felt her fist balling up; she wanted to punch one of these stupid bitches. "Ms. St. Federica, thanks for speaking with me today. Why are you ladies out here in this horridly hot weather."

Mirabel was repulsed when she saw a face so tightly stretched that it made Ms. St. Federica's lips curl up at the edges into a constant little smile and her artificial face did not have a drop of perspiration on it.

When Ms. St. Federica spoke a cruel and rough voice came through those curled lips. "We're here today because this so called America Hero broke the legs of a woman and was not arrested. Female abuse in this country is at an all-time high and something has to be done about it."

Mirabel couldn't control her anger. "Ms. St Federica are you referring to the report where a Miss Bunny Smith publicly cursed this man, spit in this man's face and then when he tried to walk away she jumped on his back and started punching him. Is this what you are protesting? Did you see this man when he was saving women and children from a burning building? Madam, in your eyes what is a hero; are you just comfortable with the cartoon heroes in the movies? This man is more than your fictional Batman, Spiderman or your mighty Superman."

Ms. St. Federica's lips were still smiling but her eyes were wide with caution and confusion. "He could have passively handled the situation."

Mirabel couldn't wait to yell, "How do you passively defend yourself when someone is on your back and punching your head. Simone, I applaud you for wanting to inform the nation about the problem of female abuse in America, but this man is a hero. Why in this country is there such an urgent need to strip our heroes of their robes of glory. Simone, take your little group of good people and go help abuse victims, actually help the victims. It's easy to protest, go and help, go and do good deeds. It's easy carrying protest signs and yelling. Roll up your sleeves and go into the community and actually help these victims. I would bet that you and your friends could be a great asset to our community. Thanks for talking with me today. Back to you Rahm."

Silence, then slowly and cautiously Rahm said, "Mirabel did I just hear you chastising that woman for protesting what she thought was female abuse. It almost sounds like you are condoning this type of behavior."

Snowy could see through the camera Mirabel's usually sun kissed complexion was now boiling red. Mirabel had been thinking about leaving WBTZ. Now she was probably going to give them no reason to keep her.

Mirabel spoke slowly and chose her words precisely. "Rahm I think your aim is to make some news instead of reporting it. I suppose you want to make WBTZ into a supermarket tabloid station like the Commercials, Nonsense and News Network.

Rahm quickly broke in, "I was just questioning your treatment of Ms. St. Federica."

Mirabel, keeping her anger internal, projected a calm exterior. "Rahm, this story is not about me and its definitely not about you. The story should only be about a man that when hell was breaking loose and everyone froze in fear and confusion, this man got off of the sidelines and stepped forward. He waded into hell to help his fellow man. That's the only story we should be reporting. So Rahm, why don't you take it to one of your precious commercials."

"I hear you Mirabel; I hear you." Rahm cleared his throat and then in a subdued voice said, "Ladies and gentlemen, we leave you for a few minutes for a station break."

Mirabel's two assistants each grasped an arm and escorted her to the air conditioned van with Eleanor bringing up the rear. Eleanor's lips were white, drained of blood because of the pressure she was applying to keep her mouth closed so that her inner rage didn't escape. If her mouth was not saying anything her wild eyes told the whole story. Eleanor stuck her head in the van and when her eyes glowing and pulsing with madness took aim at their target she let loose her pent-up fury. "What an inept amateur. In a span of a few hours you've managed to be over an hour late for work. You probably at this moment have the Black Nation in protest and boycotting WBTZ. You manage to scold, berate and criticize women who are concerned about female abuse. God knows what kind of hell that will bring the station. Then to top it all, you manage to insult on air an experienced and well respected news anchor. Then to put a cherry on top of your crazy crap you insult a national news organization. We are going to the police commissioner's update. If you have a shred of professionalism left, please use it to get through this last segment."

Mirabel's assistants had closed the van's curtains, stripped her of her sweat soaked shirt and bra and had given her a towel to dry off. She was putting on her new bra when Eleanor stuck her head into the van to yell her tirade. Eleanor caught Mirabel in a vulnerable moment; but not for long. Sitting in the back of the van attired in a fresh white bra she was ready to counterattack. Calmly Mirabel smiled at Eleanor and said,

"Eleanor I'm really sorry if I've embarrassed you. But I want to report the news. I don't want to give road side interviews to every idiot that claims to be a victim of some perceived slight. America needs heroes; we don't need to create more stories by interviewing everyone with a grievance. These people don't appreciate what our hero did, they can't see beyond their scorn. Have we just become a nation of victims, populated by a people that are angry because the world has not responded to their perceived insults, their disappointments, their rejections? I don't want our world to only have sports or cinematic make believe heroes. Are we a generation of complainers that dwells in imaginary courage because they put a bold statement on their car bumper or their T shirt or their protest placards? Yes Eleanor I have a tiny shred of professionalism left and I will use all of it to get us through the rest of the day."

Eleanor unused to being lectured smiled and took a deep breath and spoke to the empty front van seat, "Mirabel the philosopher. I don't know whether to love you or hate you." Looking at Snowy she said, "Snowy get her to our next destination and tell her about reality." Eleanor abruptly left and marched to her waiting car. She opened the passenger side door, but just stared for a few reflective moments at the network van and then her face changed back into its business mask and then she was gone.

Mirabel put on a crisp white shirt, sank into the van seat and closed her eyes as her assistants fixed her hair and make-up. Snowy drove in silence but continually looked in the rear view mirror to keep an eye on Mirabel. Snowy's steady crystalline words pierced the silence. "Mirabel are you O.K.?"

Mirabel didn't answer right away. She wasn't sure how to answer that question. "I'm fighting with Mr. Doubt. You've always said that doubting can be used to fine tune your actions; but be careful because Mr. Doubt can be a strong and corrosive opponent. Well I'm afraid he has a strong grip on me at this moment. Snowy did I do wrong today; was I that horrible? I was an amateur."

Snowy guided the van into a no parking lane, put the van in park and turned to face Mirabel and her two assistants. "Mirabel everyone loves you because you speak from your gut. You say what millions of others think but don't have the courage to say. They can see that you are honest, that you aren't harboring any hidden agendas. Oh, I'm sure you have many people doing a hilarious war dance calling for your execution. But I would bet you have many more people saying, "You go Girl." You're a good person and your kind friend, the camera, is able to let that goodness shine. I would bet even Rahm is secretively envious of you. Leave Mr. Doubt on this curb and lets go kick butt."

Mirabel closed her watery eyes and a few tears dripped off her cheek. When she opened her eyes a smile spread across her face and with her voice cracking, "Thank you Snowy. Thank you white man." She took a deep breath and said, "Lets go kick butt."

Snowy broke a few speed limits, because he knew they couldn't be late again.

Eleanor was in the parking area pointing to the location where she wanted Snowy to park the van. Before Snowy could turn off the engine, Eleanor opened the passenger door and was already giving commands. "Snowy we're going to let Pete shoot the whole briefing. We're going to carry it live. You can scout out a good spot for Mirabel to give a rehash of the briefing. Mirabel you stay in the air conditioning until we call for you. You can follow the briefing on your tablet or you can access it on the van's video monitor. Take notes and be ready to give a general overview of the meeting. Karen Kimball is working the desk because Rahm is refusing to work with you. She's been instructed to keep the questions and chit chat to a minimum. Any questions? None, well get to work."

It had been four days since the terrorist attack. The city and the nation wanted answers. The police department always wanted to report only facts and never any conjecture. Because they wanted to get everything correct before they gave any information to the public, their investigation had produced very few answers to all the obvious questions. There was a city of foreign and domestic newspaper, radio and television reporters, cameramen and satellite trucks and everyone was suffering in the midday's fierce moist heat. The mist had stopped falling but the thick clouds hung motionless. People were craving answers and the media was going to attempt to satisfy their needs. Mirabel and her two assistants followed the police commissioner's report. She took notes on everything he said. She wanted to be ready. She wanted to be professional.

Snowy's location for Mirabel's wrap up of the briefing was away from the crowds. He wanted a close up of Mirabel with the PD's head-quarters in the distant background. He had considered rigging lights because of the lack of natural light, then reconsidered thinking the unusual horrid weather should be part of the story.

Mirabel was standing where Snowy had positioned her; she was rereading her notes. She wanted to finish the day professionally but something that was said at the end of the police briefing now had her emotions rising and falling. She had the beginnings of a scream in the pit of her stomach and it was taking much of her concentration to keep it buried. The heat was no longer a factor for her; it fact she was feeling a little chill. Mirabel could see Eleanor parting the crowd as she walked directly toward her and thought the woman must have been in the military because Eleanor didn't so much walk as she marched.

Eleanor's jaw had loosened a bit and as she spoke she had a small forced smile, "Karen will be ready for you in about two minutes. Just give a brief wrap-up of the major facts and then a short commentary if you have anything, but no drama. Let's finish the day strong."

As Eleanor was backing away she could hear in her earpiece Karen introducing her, "Our correspondent Mirabel Gaspar, who has been following this story from the very beginning was at the Police Commissioner's briefing. Mirabel it looks like the police department finally has some answers for us and also some shocking revelations."

Mirabel let herself breath and with a serious expression, her golden brown eyes looked directly into the camera. "Yes Karen, in this mean, exhausting heat with these gloomy menacing clouds that stalk us this day has just gotten even darker, bitter, frustrating. The Commissioner gave us lots of information in just a twenty two minute briefing. His update was succinct but very informative. I was a bit surprised by the numbers. We had estimated twelve casualties and heard rumors of up to twenty seven. The actual numbers are thirty two dead and forty four people needing hospital care. Thirty one of those people have been released from the hospital. Six more victims are due to be release in the next couple of days. Seven of the victims of the attack are in critical care. At the time of the attack there were organizations holding meetings, there were classes and social gatherings. The Commissioner estimates that there were over four hundred people in the TJ at the time of the attack. He said that, without a doubt, if the man that they are still calling John Doe had not become involved and caused the terrorists to defend themselves instead of continuing on their killing spree, there could have been hundreds of casualties. There were six terrorists. Five of the terrorist were from North Africa and one was from Spain, who had been living in the United States for eleven years. Various terrorist groups are claiming credit for the attack. The FBI has not yet determined which group has committed this cowardly act or their motive. Of course we have learned over the years that these motherless fiends of Lucifer need no motive to satisfy their lust for blood. The Commissioner said that he would release names, including John Doe's name at tomorrow's briefing. Twice the Commissioner said that John Doe was a hero and as he was saying this there were the usual loons on the fringe carrying their placards with the words American Hero slashed through with red paint and written below was American Villain. Yes, American Villain, the Commissioner said that tomorrow John Doe will be arrested and taken into custody. I'm not sure of the timeline, but it seems that our Mystery Man was living in a quiet neighborhood in Thibodaux, Louisiana, when new neighbors wreaked havoc in the neighborhood. A young couple and the wife's brother moved into the neighborhood and decided to run it like their fiefdom. When a neighbor complained about loud music the husband and brother beat up the neighbor claiming self-defense, since the neighbor came into their yard. They threw their trash into others yards and told them to deal with it. When neighbors sat and visited on their front porches, these new neighbors accused them of spying and threatened to kill them if the police came to their house again. Those three nightmarish neighbors were found on their kitchen floor dead from gunshot wounds to the head. Three weeks later our man moved. Authorities in Louisiana now say they have evidence that he may be the assassin."

The mist returned as a drizzle and thunder that sounded like a heavy wooden desk being dragged over concrete made everyone look skyward. One of Mirabel's assistants gave her an umbrella to shield her from the drizzle. Snowy zoomed in so that Mirabel's face would fill everyone's TV screen. The close up showed a wet tired but beautiful face with thick damp hair starting to stick to her cheeks. Then he zoomed back out again so that the TV audience could see that the drizzle had turned into a light silent rain.

Mirabel paused for a second then looked away from the camera and then looked back at the camera but not directly into the lens. "I have a feeling of inexplicable loss. In America, is the Age of Heroes over? To some he was never a hero; he was just another man they could sketch in dark shades or slew with their righteous hatred. To me a solid strong oak has fallen in the savage uncaring forest. On a day when there was carnage, screams, gunfire, explosions and death, I saw courage. Hero, Good Samaritan, Solomon, the Stranger, Paul Galeo, Mystery Man, John Doe, Peter Nazreth, Miracle Man, Ahab and now Villain all names given to a most uncommon man. This may be only a few of the names in his veiled labyrinthine life. But I will only ever have one name for him- American Hero. Back to you Karen."

Mirabel pulled her earpiece from her ear, handed her assistant the umbrella and smiled at Snowy as they walked shoulder to shoulder in the warm rain.

❖

Two years later: Oscar winner for the best documentary: "The Mediterranean Cauldron: Wars and Revolutions and Social Change surrounding the Sea" Produced and directed by Snowy (W.J.) and Mirabel Landry.

Security cameras filmed in the early morning hours of May 8, the day he was to be arrested, John Doe the Mystery Man, the Hero, and two unidentified masked individuals jumping out of a second floor window at St. Joseph Hospital. Sightings of this man have been reported all over the world.

October 2013

ADDICTED

"You nervous again?" said the always friendly stage hand.
"I'm O.K."

This has been my routine, pacing near the stage curtain in this dimly lit corner of the backstage. I can't help the anxiousness and the eventual total panic that grabs hold of my body and mind minutes before my stage call. I can't explain the deep dark dungeon of my pathology; nor can I ever permanently escape it. But it is part of the fix of the short-lived high that I can't stop chasing. Even when the buzz is disappointing, I'm already thinking of the next high.

Big Alphonse the stage manager and emcee stuck his head around the corner and said, "Thirty minutes." This is always the signal for my mind to start losing control and for me to double the pace of my breathing exercises. Every time I perform, I briefly remember the day I got hooked. I was young and had never experienced the center of attention. The laughter, the smiles, the faces all contorted into a happy moving mask, was so exciting. I could feel a rushing pulse from below the belt, up my spine, and then encasing my brain in a thrilling crispness. At first it was embarrassing having people witness such a personal thrilling moment. My body and my mind were awake and functioning at high speed. It must be the same for those reckless adrenaline junkies. At the time, I didn't realize that I would spend most of my life chasing this hormonal reaction. When I was younger, the high was burning hot, but after that fleeting moment there was only emptiness. I still laugh at my decision on how to get a constant supply of captured audiences, to get a fix, when needed. Becoming a teacher was great at first, it satisfied my need, but it became way too much work and often not very fulfilling.

Suddenly Big Alphonse's big boulder head blocking the only light, yelled, "Twenty minutes. You O.K. You look like a wreck."

I better get some water; my throat is getting a little parched. My breathing exercise dries the back of my throat. I always remind myself not to swallow the water because of my fear of vomiting on stage. As I've gotten older, I have lessened my need for my fix. Actually I have begun to enjoy the coming down, the withdrawal, more than the high. If all goes well my reward has become a comfortable place with a cup of coffee and a couple of cigarettes. Age the big killer of a wanton appetite has taken over my body.

Ten sausage fingers came around the corner before Big Alphonse's searching eyes found me and then his thick bulbous lips mouthed the word ten. I can feel my body going into a manic anxiousness. The flight hormone is really kicking in and my heart is racing; but I can feel my emotions moving my arms and legs in adagio. The edges of my peripheral vision are shaded. I can see clearer, inward. I feel like I am drowning in saliva. The more I swallow the faster the refill comes. I can taste a metallic tension. Once again my emotions are trying to monster me. The bottom of my stomach is doing its usual dance of pain. This is crazy; why do I do this to myself? I can feel my insides shaking. It would be so easy to walk out the back door, go home and take a warm comforting bath.

I can hear Big Al asking the audience to give a big hand for the sketch comedians that had just performed. I can barely hear my name as I am introduced. The terror has almost paralyzed me. As I walk out onto the stage my legs are so stiff I must look like a robot. I wear the black velvet slippers so that my feet can slide across the stage floor with a minimum of effort. I know my voice will crack in the beginning, but if I can hold it together for a few minutes I will be just fine. I am already sweating profusely.

"Good Evening Ladies and Gentlemen. Big Al introduced me as the man from the bayous of Louisiana. He said I was a Louisiana Cajun. What is a Cajun?"

Someone yells, "Swamp man."

"Good job, good answer. Cajuns actually were peasants that came from the central western region of France in the sixteen hundreds and settled the Acadia area of Canada which is now called Nova Scotia. These people had always been tied to the brutal old-world feudalism. But now they were free farmers and fishermen. When the English took over part of Canada they confiscated the Acadian's land and exiled them out of Canada. This is called the Cajun Exodus. Moses had nothing on the Cajuns. Eventually they settled on the Louisiana prairies, near swamps and in my ancestors' case along Bayou Lafourche. As Cajuns, everywhere we go we are asked questions about our culture. So we invented two characters that are a good representation of many good-hearted Cajuns. Their names are Boudreaux and Thibodaux. So that's why I am here tonight, to tell you some stories about Boudreaux and Thibodaux and hopefully these stories will give you a better understanding of Cajun culture."

"One day Thibodaux is walking down the banquette. A banquette is what you call a sidewalk." Someone yells, "Why don't you just say sidewalk?"

When Thibodaux gets to Boudreaux's house he sees Boudreaux sitting on his porch with two swollen black eyes and he says, "May Boudreaux how ya got those two black eyes."

Boudreaux's swollen bruised eyes barely showed a sliver of eyeball. With a serious and somewhat mystified look he said to Thibodaux, "May ah was in church minding my own business. Ah was kneeling in the pew and then Father Breaux called us to come up for the communion. There was dis big, big girl in the pew in front of me and when she stood up her dress caught between those big fluffy cheeks. Her dress was being eaten. Ah couldn't let that poor girl embarrass herself; so ahs reached in and pulled out her dress. That crazy girl turned around and booms, she hit me in my eye."

Thibodaux laughing so hard he can barely say, "Well Boudreaux what about your other eye?"

Boudreaux slowly shook his head back and forth and with a sly smile said, "May ahs figured that's the way she wanted it so I stuck it back in." With that last statement and his hand slowly going into imaginary pillows of flesh, the audience roared with laughter.

I am going to be O.K. I can already feel the rush. I need to keep them a little longer to get the full high. I need more of their energy. I'm gonna be O.K. I feel like I could fight a duel, fearless. I'm going to use them. Give it to them fast. Give them very little time to think. Stop or slow down when you want them to think, guide them.

"Now let me tell you what happened when my ancestors arrived in Louisiana. First, the Indians said, "There goes the neighborhood." The creole French in the big city of New Orleans were like nobility to the penniless country-less refugees from Canada. But these refugees were hard workers; they had carved out a living in the harsh winter climate of the Canadian Maritime provinces and now the Acadians were going to live again as free farmers along the bayous and prairies of southern Louisiana. Over time the name Acadians was shortened to les cadiens and eventually to Cajun. Let me tell you another story about Boudreaux and Thibodaux."

"Boudreaux and Thibodaux were choupicing near Lake Verrett. A choupic is a long green slightly slimy, slippery fish. They were on a chenier fishing with cane poles in an amber tea colored bayou. Suddenly Boudreaux screams. Thibodaux jumped to catch up with his heart and said, "What the hell Boudreaux?"

Boudreaux was bent over at the waist, pale faced with a look of shock mixed with pain and a trembling voice said, "When I squatted a water moccasin bit me. He bit my manhood right on da head. What ahms I gonna do, Thibodaux?"

Thibodaux now in his superman mode and using his hands to put emphasis on his words said, "Stay calm, ahs going to run to town and get Dr. Molaison to help you." When Thibodaux got to Dr. Molaison's office, he ran through the waiting room straight into the examing room where he found Dr. Molaison with a half-naked patient. Thibodaux could barely speak because he was so out of breath but grabbed Dr. Molaison by the arm and was able to mutter, "Dr. Mo, Boudreaux, bitten by a cotton mouth, come."

Dr. Molaison said, "Ahs got the pneumonia and after ahs help Miss Gloria with her stress ahs got to go home and rest."

Thibodaux in stunned silence looks at Dr. Mo, then Miss Gloria, then back to Dr. Mo and says, "You got to help me."

Dr. Molaison said, "Ahs gonna tell you what to do. It's easy. First you gotta take one hand and hold steady the area were Boudreaux was bitten. Then you gots to wrap your lips around the wound and suck."

Thibodaux wide eyed and shaking his head no said, "Ahs don't know Dr. Mo."

Dr. Molaison shoving Thibodaux out of the door said, "You can do it. Just suck hard and don't forget to spit."

Thibodaux crimson-faced stood in the waiting room for a minute to think, shook his head in disgust and took off running. Thibodaux found Boudreaux lying down and in a lot of pain.

When Boudreaux saw Thibodaux with renewed strength he stood up and said, "May wheres Dr. Mo? What dat doc says?"

Thibodaux with a look of sadness said, "Boudreaux, Dr. Mo said you gonna die. He said you gonna die.""

The sudden roar of laughter, the riff is so electric. I'm steering my instrument to carry me to a new and clean high. I feel awake. I feel deliriously uninhibited. Now I am kicking; thank you God. I'm alive. I knew when there was a long eager silence that I had won and then the anticipated roar was all the better. I can feel it at the tip of my spine. My toes are gripping my shoe soles.

"Thank You. Boudreaux and Thibodaux, they are always getting into innocent trouble. Just like most Cajuns, they get knocked down and they get back up. They were peasants in France. Then they were hard working free farmers in Acadia. Knocked down by the British and exiled from their homes; they successfully carved out a living in the Louisiana wilderness. How about another Boudreaux story?"

A police officer pulled over Boudreaux who had been weaving in and out of traffic. He walked up to the car and said, "Sir, I need you to blow is this breathalyzer tube."

"Ahm sorry, officer, but ah can't do that. Cuz me, ahm an asthmatic. If ah try ta do dat, ahm goin' have me a bad asthma attack."

"O.K., then I'll need you to come down to the station to give a blood sample," said the officer.

"Yabbut ah can't do that nedda," said Boudreaux. "Ya see, ahm a hemophiliac and wit any little cut ah could bleed ta deat.

Now the police officer very irritated says, "We'll need you to come to the station to give a urine sample."

Boudreaux looking a little sheepish said, "Ahm so sorry but dat's out of dat question. You see. Ahm a diabetic and if ah do dat ahm goin' git really low blood sugar."

Now the officer screaming, "Get out of that car and walk that white line."

"May ah can't do dat nedda," said Boudreaux raising his voice.

"Why not?" yelled the officer.

"Maaay, cuz ahm drunk, me!" said Boudreaux. Loud laughter and applause and many in the audience saying, "Maaay, cuz ahm drunk, me." I'm there, the full syringe. This is supremo stuff. Cheaper than I expected. I can barely hear them. "No drinking and driving; not even for Boudreaux. People seem to think that before the civil war that everyone down south had slaves. Maybe they did, I couldn't tell you about other places but I know that there were very few slaves along Bayou Lafourche until a man by the name of Etienne de Bore discovered the process of crystalizing sugar. Sugar became very profitable and Louisiana was a great place for growing sugar cane. Americans began arriving in the bayou region buying up huge swaths of land and importing slaves for cheap labor on these massive plantations. The Cajuns were happy to sell their land. They had always been subsistence farmers and now they had money in their hands. Their rural innocence brought them no land and soon no money. So let me tell you what Boudreaux thinks about that."

Boudreaux and Thibodaux were sitting at the bar in Charlo's Bar getting "chockayed." Thibodaux said, "Boudreaux, watcha tink about dem term limits for politicians?"

"Maaay, ahm all in favor of dat," said Boudreaux.

"How come?" said Thibodaux.

Boudreaux looking up at the ceiling in contemplation, "Ah tink dem politicians ought ta be changed on a regular basis, jis like a little baby's diaper and fo da seem reason." The applause is still there, but now some members of the audience are standing up to applaud and whooping shouts. Adrenaline high, I'm almost finished. I felt the excited tingle and now the creeping euphoric state. "The Cajuns were glad when the Civil War was over because many former slaves left the bayou and so now they could get jobs to replace the slaves on the plantations that were once their land. Like all ethnic groups, after each new generation the Cajuns became Americanized and have lost touch with much of their culture. I want to thank you for being a great audience and for giving mc a high that you could never imagine. I want to give you one more Boudreaux story and one of my favorite stories."

"Thibodaux, Boudreaux, Nelson and Randy are sitting on Boudreaux's front porch drinking homemade blackberry wine when Thibodaux said, "Ya'll ever wonder what people goona say at your eulogy."

Nelson with blackberry stained lips belched, "He was a hardworking good man, simple aze dat."

Randy already feeling the effects of the first glass of wine said, "May, ah hope they say. There goes da best dam hunter in all of Louisiana."

Thibodaux proud of his long thought out eulogy and with a drunken smile said, "Ahs hope day say, he was a good fartha, good grandfartha, good great grandfartha, good great, great grandfartha and so on. And din ahs want them to say how smart ahs was."

Boudreaux in deep focused concentration took his finger way from his lips and said, "Not me, ahs want them to approach my coffin and with big eyes and their hair standing straight at attention say, "Look! Look, maay he's moving."

The crowd enjoying themselves gave a loud applause. A short salute is given in appreciation to their willingness to enjoy and in turn make it enjoyable for me. Alphonse making his stage entrance, stuck out a hand and when I gripped it he said, "Good job Wayne, you always hookem." In my euphoric arousal, I can only nod my head and smile. Backstage, members of the sketch comedian troupe pat me on my back and praise me. Tonight's major act, the now famous Steve Fish came over for a congratulatory handshake. I'm not sure what he said because all I can feel is a huge sense of satisfaction. My legs feel so loose, so light, so flexible. I call them my Elvis Presley legs, my stride is elastic, but my velvet slippers know where to take me. I'm hypnotized by the eerily calmness that I feel; which is usually a stranger to me.

As I enter Sally's Maison de Coffee and Garden, I seek my cave, my security, my box seat for the coming human dramas. There in the far corner of the garden is my destination and good; my favorite waiter, always in a dark mood and consistently indignant, is working tonight.

In the far corner of the garden where the light comes so close to penetrating the darkness, all that can be seen is swirling smoke as it fogs up the seeking light and a white coffee cup tilted into darkness.

May 2011

JUST TRYING TO GET BY

Seated in his comfortable throne, he was thinking about the jury that he had asked for, he knew these twelve people were his only chance. He knew he was as good as any D.A. carnivore. He could read people and he understood how to stroke them and when to win them over to his point of view. He was an entertainer and when he had to, he could entertain. He enjoyed all people, but women were his specialty. He seldom had an unemployed erection because women always enjoyed his company. He could make a policeman give him another chance, even when the cop knew he was making a mistake. He always said that he was just a simple fisherman; an apostle with faith in his silken net. The fish and the fisherman both enjoying the mental euphoria of the struggle. He liked his chances and if he could bet and he would bet if he could, he would put all the marbles on himself. Looking out of the police van he said, "Hey Officer Jonathan, drive slow. Let's enjoy this beautiful sunny, soft blue day. Louisiana in October is a short glimpse of Paradise. No humidity. Let's say that again Mr. Jonathan. No damn humidity." Officer Jonathan smiled, but never made eye contact, because he knew the man's powers. With a love-for-life smile he soaked in the positive energy of the day. "No humidity, a cool breeze, a friendly sun and let's not forget dead-ass mosquitoes," he said to no one in particular. Seeing two attractive women walking on the sidewalk he said, "Officer Jonathan slow down. Let's enjoy the view. Check out these two pretend Madonnas."

Officer Jonathan looked into the rearview mirror and saw him sitting in the last seat, with that smile. "Hey man, I got to get you guys to court by eight o'clock. I don't know why, because everyone just walks around like lost souls in black and white. Everyone walks around with a satisfied grin on their face and then suddenly, with no warning, a mad dash in third gear and if I haven't delivered the prisoners, then my nuts are in the cracker."

Locking on to Officer Jonathan's eyes that had strayed too long in the mirror, his friendly smile burned, "I understand my brother, I understand."

The van pulled up to the New Orleans City Court and his smile turned to a snarl and said, "This ugly-ass building. New Orleans is old brick and eaten timber. Rotting and sinking sometimes gracefully and sometimes well not so gracefully. This fortress, this gray stone behemoth just doesn't belong here, maybe New York or Russia, but not in the Big Easy."

Officer Jonathan opened the van door and said, "OK guys, lets hop to it. We're on a tight schedule." Two prisoners file out of the van, then he stepped out and unfolded himself into a position of an alert security dog. Eyes watching everything, missing nothing and that constant inviting smile waiting for his chance.

Officer Jonathan closed the van door, turned, and said, "Good luck guys. Hey Razor, this is it. Good Luck man. Ya'll, this is Officer Gloria Hebert, and she will take you to your assigned court rooms."

Officer Hebert with a tight smile pointed to a door, "Alright guys I need you to line up single file and walk to that side door left of the main doors."

Razor visually stripping Officer Hebert, "Gloria lets stand for a while in this beautiful sun and smoke a cigarette."

Officer Hebert caught him checking out her body, "I don't smoke, let's keep moving."

Razor mentally thanking Gloria for wearing pants so tight, so nasty delicious, "Gloria I bet you smoke. I bet you look hot experiencing the rush from exhaling. Gloria, could you stand to the side and give us a profile. We want to envision you smoking."

Gloria liked the attention, at least he wasn't angry and rude like most of the prisoners, smiled and met his gaze, "Get in line and behave like your friends."

Sensing an opening, Razor said, "You're the most beautiful thing I've seen all week."

Gloria's smile vaporized and her brows furrowed, "Did you say thing?"

Shocked at his poor choice of words Razor thinks to himself "Watch yourself; you are going to be challenged by people that are probably a lot smarter than Gloria. Remember stay calm, don't be defensive, be on the offense and watch for any openings and definitely don't say something stupid." Recovering from his sloppy word play, Razor's handsome gregarious grin flirted with Officer Gloria, "I'm so stunned by a beauty in uniform that I couldn't deliver the proper flower."

Officer Hebert liked this cocky flirt, he was handsome and silly. She thought he probably was a good guy. He was like her, just trying to make a little money to pay for her few expenses. Most likely he had been minding his own business; just trying to get by. She appreciated being called a beauty in uniform, but knew that her uniform didn't fit properly and her hair, her poor hair, who could afford it.

Laughing, Razor nudges the prisoner in front of him and says, "Blaine tell her to give us a smoke."

Blaine looking a little aggravated says, "Yeh, she's going to let me lick her ass before she lets us smoke a cigarette. You better start getting serious."

The prisoners walked through the huge metal green court-room doors and are hit with a body stiffening chill. Razor looking, searching, lets out a little tremor and says, "Damn it's cold in here. This would have been inviting on a day with ninety-two degree heat and one hundred percent humidity." Razor always blamed the grip of heavy weather on people's crazy behavior. Summertime heat and humidity makes you feel sticky, then dirty and if you are unfortunate to look into a mirror and see a shiny greasy face and a really embarrassing head of hair, then you begin to break down and loose some inhibitions. It's not long before everyone with you looks and smells like a zoological crazy. Then the craziness begins and before long you don't care. Razor had experienced the soft and elusive sunshine of northern Europe, the blazing brightness of the Middle East and the California glow but there was only one place where the sunshine felt familiar, felt like home, like a friend. The Sun's rays that warmed the earth around Thirty Degrees north and between Ninety and Ninety One Degrees West brought comfort to Razor's mind, the shades, and the shadows were just right.

The line of prisoners stop in front of courtroom 3A and Gloria looked on her clip board and said, "Mr. Jean Philippe Landry courtroom number 3A."

Razor was surprised to hear his name. Everyone knew him as Razor. His Grandfather had given him the name because he said he was sharper than a tack and always on a razor's edge between good and bad. Since the age of eight, family, friends, teachers, enemies, the Law, his women, bosses, all knew him as Razor.

"Officer Gloria I don't want a three, I need a seven or an eleven."

Smiling and cheeks blushing Gloria was enjoying her morning, "I'm sorry, but I don't assign courtrooms. Good luck Mr. Landry."

Razor knew he had already made a friend, "Everyone calls me Razor."

"Why Razor?"

Razor with a slightly more serious smile said, "I will be through with this silliness very soon and then maybe dinner and I can explain why Razor." Then slowly and measured he said with a sly smile, "Then after dinner maybe you could arrest me."

Razor turned and entered the court room and immediately saw a young rumpled stranger smiling and walking towards him. Razor thinking to himself, "Do I know this guy?"

The young stranger extended his hand for a handshake, "Hello Mr. Laundry."

Looking over the puffy, poorly dressed hair plant Razor did not offer his hand, said, "Landry, its Landry. Are you Steve Boudreaux's assistant?"

The young stranger withdrew his empty hand and deposited it in his pants pocket, then nervously mumbled, "My name is Robby Lee. Mr. Boudreaux is dead, I'll explain that latter. I am your new court appointed attorney."

Razor's face contorted into a mask of shock. "Oh fuck! This is bad! This is a disaster. This is bad fucking karma."

The young man's face burned a blotchy red and when he started to speak Razor put his hands up to silence him. After a few seconds of silent thought, Razor placed his attention on the young man, squinted his green eyes as if to bring his thoughts into clearer focus and said, "What's your name?"

"Robby Lee."

Razor's hands still saying silence, his jaw set and tight, "OK, Rudy, the first thing you have to do is get the judge to postpone the trial."

Robby Lee looking like a fat kid slowly backing away from the end of a diving board blurted, "I can't do that. Judge Magotcha would never postpone this trial. She probably thinks these proceedings won't last an hour."

In a menacing gravelly baritone voice Razor pointed a finger at the young lawyer and said, "Rudy if you are going to be my lawyer you will do two things. One, get this trial postponed now and two, do something with your damn ridiculous hair."

"My hair, what's the matter with my hair?"

"No one sees anything but that pile of rubble on top of your head. It makes you look like an in-between with a bad wig."

His mouth open in shock and embarrassment said, "I won't even ask what an in-between is and my name is Robby." Licking his lips, Robby realized that this case might not be as easy as he had thought mumbled, "Mr. Landry we really don't want to get this judge upset. I've studied Mr. Boudreaux's notes regarding your case. You've been identified by three eye-witnesses and may I emphasize that there was a security camera in the vicinity that shows a man of your size in the area at the time of the crime. All you can really do is plead guilty and hope for leniency. We definitely do not want to anger this judge."

His lowered brow shaded his usually bright and alert eyes, Razor's face frozen in contemplation turned to the young lawyer and said, "Rudy, get away from me, let me think."

"Mr. Landry, they don't have jail house snitches, they have three real eye witnesses."

A sneer spreading across his face, Razor put his hand on the young lawyer's shoulder and laughed, "Call me Razor." Looking past the young lawyer's shoulder, staring at his plan running through his mind, his hand tightened on the young man's shoulder. He flashed a brotherly smile and said, "Rudy we can do this. Don't tell me what to do, but help me do what I have to do. Do you understand; I do not lie down and quit. I definitely don't let other people tell me to lie down and quit. Work with me Rudy and I'll make you a winner today. How many cases have you won?"

"I've only been involved with four cases and I have successfully completed each case."

"How many did you win and kept your client out of jail?"

Robby Lee with a sheepish smile said, "None."

Out the corner of his eye Razor saw a well-dressed familiar face approach, "Hello Mr. Lee, I don't think we've met. My name is Bob Rome. I will be the lead prosecutor today." Turning to Razor with serious politeness he said, "Hello Razor, how are you doing?" Razor with a shimmer in his eye light smiled, "Hello Bob, like everyone else I'm just trying to get by."

Bob Rome turned to Robby Lee and with a wink, "Mr. Lee is there anything you need to tell me?"

Robby Lee looking celebrity shocked blurted out, "No. I mean, ahm, not now. Maybe, maybe later."

Sizing up the competition Razor stares at the prosecuting team, "So Bobby Rome, the District Attorney himself, will be the lead prosecutor. Why so much fire power? This can't be good. He never loses. He'll cross boundaries that might not even be legal. He knows it's always easier to say that you are so very sorry. He's got that movie star look. Those kinds of good looks can do wonders for you if you know how to use them. A position to envy. Gleaming Prick."

Recovering his composure Robby Lee asked, "Do you know the D.A.?"

"Unfortunately I know almost everyone in the District Attorney's office."

Turning to face the prosecuting team Razor nods toward the attractive blonde in a rather tight black dress, "That's Candy Clemens. Candy, what an appropriate name. Look at that onion booty."

Robby mesmerized by the blonde said, "What?"

"Rudy, an onion booty is a booty that's so fine it makes you want to cry. See how she's walking on her toes for us."

Robby already under her spell, "Those are called high heels. Ooh, bella vista."

Stepping into his line of vision Razor stares into Robby's eyes, "No, no Rudy she's walking on her toes for you and me. Bob Rome knows what he is doing. She's our distraction while Bob Rome is castrating us. Do not look at her. Do not even venture a peek. We have a serious job. After we win, then we can play."

Robby Lee and Razor sat at the defendant's table and huddled, "O.K. Rudy, this is Plan A. All I need from you is to get me on the stand and keep asking questions about me. Let me talk to the jury. I have to make them think that I am one of them. Don't lead me into pity. Make it into an us against them situation. I'll put them in my shoes; I'll make their eyes reveal to me what they don't want to reveal and then I'll show them that I understand. Eight women and four men on the jury. I'll dance to "A Whiter Shade of Pale" with each one. The men will be easy."

With a confused smile Robby put his hand to his forehead and slowly shook his head, "That's Plan A. What's Plan B? The D.A. won't let me keep you up there to talk about your problems. You're talking about a cocktail party. If you got a Plan B, tell me now."

A side door opened and out walked the jury. Razor, standing at attention, looked at each member of the jury like a fox appraising his meal. He knew these twelve people would determine his fate. It didn't matter what the judge or the district attorney thought or said; it all depended on the emotions of these twelve people.

The bailiff appeared and shouted, "All rise for the Honorable Judge Serena Magotcha."

In walked a tired, blonde-dyed, middle aged stone face wearing a black robe that was so big that it brought a smile to everyone's face. Razor studied her face for any sign of emotion. People like Judge Magotcha had always intrigued him. People like the Judge never see humans; they never focus on one person. Razor had seen that stare many times before. The stare that says I will not see you until I am ready for you. She had a laser focus and hints of anger that led you to believe the rumors of her being a descendent of Torquemada.

He turned to the young lawyer, eager to get started, Razor said, "I can crack this nut. Listen, Rudy, does the prosecutor start first?"

Robby Lee staring quizzically at Razor said, "Of course."

With a firm grip on the young lawyer's shoulder and a finger point at his chest, the words rapidly spilled out of Razor's mouth, "Let him speak for a few minutes and then I want you to stand up and say that if you believe him to be guilty put Mr. Landry on the stand. Then I will take it from there."

Robby Lee with fear in his eyes and in a hushed deep voice, "Are you crazy? I can't do that. That's not the proper procedure. The judge will provide you with a new lawyer before lunch if I make such a drastic breach of protocol."

Razor's hand moved to the back of the young lawyer's neck and pulled him face to face and firmly said, "Rudy, I'm gonna punch you in the mouth and I can guarantee that before the bailiff can stop me I will knock teeth out of your mouth. You work for me; so do what I say. Hell, Rudy we both know, you're not a good lawyer. This can be the excuse to get out of this life-sapping job. On the other hand, following my directions might light a fire under your unhealthy ass and in victory you may impress the onion booty."

Robby Lee could feel his hair getting damp, "Or maybe make a fool of myself, get arrested and thrown in jail for contempt. Yes, it would be very impressive walking out of court in handcuffs with my teeth in my hands."

Judge Magotcha swinging her head side to side to get her long dead hair out of her face grumbled, "Counselors please approach the bench."

Robby Lee walked on wobbly legs to the bench. As for as the judge was concerned he could have been the Invisible Man; but when Mr. America approached the bench marble-faced Serena chiseled a smile for the D.A.

Razor realized that Bob the Bastard, in his relationship with the judge, had a strong advantage. He turned to analyze and dissect his jury. He quickly realized that each jury member was transfixed on the D.A. He cleared his throat to get their attention or just to break their stare. No one turned to even notice him sitting there in the courtroom. He wiped a little brook of sweat from his upper lip and felt his stomach get roller-coaster sick. Razor could feel his confidence quickly retreating, like an army in rout.

Robby Lee walked back to the defendant's table observed Razor and with a worried look said, "Mr. Landry what's the matter? You suddenly look very sick. Are you feeling O.K.?"

Razor responds half heartily, "Call Me Razor."

Robby Lee slowly and drawn out says, "Raazoor."

Looking into the distance Razor said, "That's my name." Turning to the young lawyer he gave a defeated smile, "O.K. Ruby it's almost time to do your thing."

The young lawyer with a heavy heart smile, "You mean Rudy."

Razor's mind shut down for a few minutes and all he could hear was some garbled statements that sounded like background music coming from the Judge and then the D.A.'s final statement, "Your Honor we will prove that Mr. Landry's repeated lapses in good judgment have become a problem for the hardworking members of our community."

With a suddenness that shocked everyone and with an absolute firmness the young lawyer shot up and said, "I object your Honor. We are only dealing with this case."

Judge Magotcha's face turned into a flesh eating barbarian looking for someone to kill. Mr. America calmly looked down at the floor and smiled. Razor's back hardened ramrod straight, his heart came out of flat line and he passed his hand through his static hair. The jury, twelve strong, their eyes glued to the D.A. never turned to see where this noise came from.

Judge Magotcha, with a seriously contorted face, spat out between clenched teeth, "Mr. Lee, never yell in this court." And then slowly, "We are only dealing with this one case."

The young lawyer slowly sat down, turned with a stiff neck and stared at Razor then gave him a wink. Razor could feel the heat from the young lawyer's part crimson and part blood-starved face. His strength replenished and his confidence restored, Razor whispered to the young lawyer, "Where'd you find those big balls?"

He was beginning to feel a little giddy. If his lawyer was ready for a fight, then it was time for him to roll up his sleeves and take it to the enemy. He rose from his chair and gave a righteous stare to the judge, "Your Honor let's just cut to the chase, let me get up there and tell you what happened and then these twelve ladies and gentlemen can make a decision and then we can all go home."

Judge Magotcha rose out of her throne and with her devil red face, only missing horns, stabbed her bony pitch-fork finger at Razor, growled for a moment, then shouted, "OH NO. WE WILL NOT HAVE THESE INTERRUPTIONS IN THIS COURT." Turning to the young lawyer, her upper lip snarling and trembling with anger came down a few decibels, "Mr. Lee do you need a few minutes to explain things to your client."

Robby Lee still stunned from Razor's actions could barely mumble, "No your Honor."

Razor turned to the jury and could feel his confidence slip away; the jury members were staring at him with eyes of contempt. He knew he had already lost his jury.

Mr. America was still looking at the floor and smiling. Judge Magotcha teepeed her hands in front of her face and closed her eyes for a second to compose herself. She had dealt with Razor before and she could always see the good in this man. Sometimes she even envied him for his freedom that came with his nothing-to-lose attitude. She knew if he'd had a different life as a child, he could easily be sitting in her chair. He was smart, people smart and had the ability and the desire to earnestly talk to everyone. He made everyone feel like they had a fresh start after conversing with him. With a better education he could have been anything, he could have taken jobs in career fields that he doesn't even know exist. His crimes were harmless to the majority of people. Yes he relieved many, many people of their money; which they knowingly and foolishly risked. He also knew and did business with many dangerous people. Maybe incarceration and education could help him. Judge Magotcha calmly took her hands from her face and said "Counselors please approach the bench."

While Mr. America and Razor's new found superhero talked with the judge he thought this might be a good time to repair the damage he inflicted on his jury. Razor turned to the jury and just saw a disaster. It is obvious that the middle aged woman in the front row is visually undressing the D.A. and for God's sake maybe even Rudy. The old alligator-skin black woman looks pissed. She'll probably convict me just because she missed the Oprah Show. The idiot on the end of the back row has locked his stare on Miss Onion Booty and the weird looking young woman sitting next to the cougar is daydreaming with an electric shocked stare. No one will venture any eye contact with him. It almost seems they were instructed to not have eye contact with the defendant.

Judge Magotcha turned to the young lawyer and before she could speak he rattled at high speed, "Why don't we give him what he wants; put him on the stand; bring in the eyewitness and then let the jury vote. Everything done in an hour, everyone happy, except probably Mr. Landry, we make room on the court docket and we save the taxpayer's unwilling charity.

The Judge raised her hairy lip in incredulous contempt and whispered to the young lawyer, "What law school did you graduate from? Mr. Lee after this case we must sit down and discuss your future in law."

Robby Lee shrank from her attack and turned to look at Razor, knowing that he was going to fail in helping this man. Less than an hour ago Razor was a stranger and now he would do anything to win this case for him. He turned back to participate in the discussion the Judge was having with the D.A. The Judge and the D.A. decided to take a short recess so that Robby could explain court procedure to his client and to wait for the eye-witnesses to arrive.

Robby had just sat down at the defendant's table when the judge realized she had forgotten to stress something to the young lawyer. Judge Magotcha spoke into her microphone, "Mr Lee can you." In mid-sentence the microphone stopped working, the lights dimmed then the courtroom went dark and the air conditioning took a big heave then said I quit. Silence, then the click of the emergency lights coming to attention put a funeral home glow to the courtroom. The Judge yelled to the people in the courtroom, "Everyone stay seated, this may just be a temporary outage."

Robby sat next to Razor nervously, hesitantly he uttered, "O.K. Razor they want to make a deal. You plead guilty. The Judge says three years because of repeated infractions and she promises to keep you out of the parish jail. There is a new state program with new facilities where you work, learn a trade, and continue your education. Go to trial and lose and she will seek the maximum."

A courtroom deputy with shirt buttons screaming to hold back the tide of belly fat ambled over to the judge and spoke to her. Judge Magotcha stood up and spoke to the courtroom, "There has been an automobile accident two blocks from the courthouse and a transformer has been knocked out, the deputy said that within twenty minutes we could have power. If anyone needs to go to the restroom or get a sip of water go now and come back immediately to your seat. We will continue as soon as power resumes."

Looking defeated, Razor turned to the young lawyer and said, "What is the maximum?"

Embarrassed, Robby muttered to himself, "Well, if she is going to give you a deal with three years, the maximum must be three to five years longer. But I'm really just guessing. Take the deal and I'd bet you a free man in two years."

Razor put his elbows on the table; cradled his chin with his right hand and went into quiet contemplation. The old dark marble courtroom felt like a dungeon. Another courtroom deputy race-walked into the courtroom and stood on his toes to speak to the Judge. The Judge sat back with consternation spread across her face. Then she waved to the D.A. and the young lawyer to approach the bench. As the three huddled and spoke, looks of astonishment hung on their faces.

In deep thought, Robby Lee slowly walked back to the defendant's table. Razor, eager to hear the news, barked, "What the hell happened?"

Bending over the table to get close to Razor, Robby whispered, "There won't be a trial."

His lips etched a quizzical smile and the shine returned to Razor's eyes; he whispered back to his lawyer, "What?"

Still trying to comprehend what he just heard, Robby said, "The three eyewitnesses were in that accident two blocks from the courthouse. They were killed."

The smile still holding the lips, his eyes narrowed to focus on the young lawyer's response to his question, "They were riding together?"

Robby Lee could see that the face, that smile, those eyes that could hypnotize most people was back. He walked around the table so that he could sit near Razor and still in a hushed tone said, "They didn't feel safe coming to the courthouse. It was decided to give the three a ride in a police van. When they stopped at a red traffic-light, a concrete truck never stopped and hit them from behind and crushed the van killing everyone."

Razor sat back into his chair, his face relaxed, a satisfied smile spread his lips, and he turned his gaze to the jury. Robby Lee sat in his chair never taking his eyes off of Razor and waited for something, waited for a reaction.

Razor turned back to his lawyer, the smile still there, spoke softly, "Cousin Wayne, he was Plan B."

November 2010

I STILL LOVE YOU

The Plan

I have been plotting, planning, calculating and saving for this project. It's been on my mind for a little over two years. Some people can't believe that I didn't complete this project two years ago. A rush to action could have been detrimental to me. Why do something if you can't do it right. A project has a beginning; the planning part, down to the smallest detail. Plan the project out and take into account any changes that may be needed to perfect the project. Then visualize the completed project and take a practice run or at least visit the areas where the project will take place to seek out any weaknesses. The last part of the project should be how to defend the project, especially to yourself. I've had some private enjoyment planning this project; at times becoming too emotionally involved. This afternoon I will start the first phase of my plan. The first phase calls for an important meeting with someone that I must convince to work for me. In just thirty minutes, at three o'clock this afternoon I will be meeting with my cousin. This cousin is a vital part of my planned project. If this meeting goes well then the project should be completed quickly and with a minimum of work or stress. This cousin is a little strange and not close to anyone in the family. I have some cousins that I can call friends; but not Susie. She really has no friends and doesn't plan for the future because she has no fanciful dreams. She is neither grateful nor sad for each day. She doesn't dwell on the past, because she realizes you can't change painful life events. I know "What You Looking At" Susie is wondering why her cousin Truc is coming to visit.

The neighborhood was built in the early to mid-fifties. The large yards have double wide shotgun houses, which were built sturdy enough to withstand hurricanes. The houses were built to raise an active family; the yards were for the wild barefoot kids. This was the neighborhood and the house that Susie's parents began their wedded bliss and now Susie lived in the house alone, no one to take care of her, no friends; just the television and the dogs.

When Truc knocked on the door, a stampede of howling dogs rushed to the door. One of the dogs took his job very serious as he was growling through the door to warn any trespassers. Truc could see Susie through the threadbare curtain covering the glassed half of the door as she slowly walked to the door. Her curly coarse golden hair was in the same style that Susie had worn as a little girl. Hairstyle, cosmetics, clothes were never a concern for Susie; she knew no expensive dress could ever help her.

Susie said something to the dogs and slowly opened the door and said, "Hello cousin."

"Hey Susie, am I on time?"

Susie, with a small tight grin, chuckled, "Anytime is on time. Come on in. Don't worry about the dogs. They are all bark and no bite."

As Truc hesitantly slipped through the door the boss dog growled and lunged at Truc. With preternatural speed, Susie grabbed the big dog by the collar, lifted his head so that he could see her face and snapped, "I said it's O.K."

Truc suddenly felt warm on this cool early October afternoon and was a little unnerved by Susie's super swift arm action. Keeping a wary eye on the boss dog he said, "Here you go Susie, I brought you some sweets from Bob's Donuts." The other two slacker dogs latched their begging eyes on the box of sweets. When Susie grabbed the box it looked like she was not looking at the box but instead was staring at the wall. Why was this handicap, this defect not taken care of when she was a child? No one ever knew what Susie was looking at. As innocent kids, Truc and the rest of the cousins would be confused by her crazily aimed eyes and always said, "What you looking at Susie?" An innocent question became a name.

Susie led him into the kitchen that he remembered from twenty years ago when he last visited Susie's parents. Turning her head to face Truc and in her monotone voice droned, "I just made a fresh pot of coffee. Would you like a cup or maybe some tea to wash down the sweets?"

Relieved to be greeted by her cordial behavior, Truc gave a quick, "Yes!"

Pointing to an old faded yellow upholstered kitchen chair she said, "Sit there." Feeling a sense of homecoming Truc sat at an early 1950's era kitchen table very much like the one his parents owned when he was very young and they were much poorer. Susie poured coffee into cups that were probably her mother's, from a vaguely familiar drip coffee pot that he was sure had been their Grandmothers. This was the exact kitchen where he had sat and drank coffee with her parents twenty years ago. The refrigerator was newer and the faded green wall coloring had been a heavily stained yellow. As Susie carefully pushed the ceramic sugar and creamer containers to Truc's side of the table and with her face pointed towards the fine antiques muttered, "How yah been?"

Truc put a spoon full of sugar into his coffee and as he stirred his coffee, for a fleeting moment he thought about unloading the truth, "I've been doing pretty good, actually I'm doing O.K."

As Susie slowly, methodically transferred the box of sweets from the stove to the table three pairs of eyes carefully and eagerly watched every step she made, mindful that anything spilt or dropped could be a nice midafternoon treat. Her eyes seemed to be looking two feet away from the desert box; she opened the gift and with the first really noticeable facial expression squealed, "Oh my god, a whole tarte ala bouillie pie." When properly motivated, Susie could move at an incredible speed. She served each of them a slice of pie on chipped dishes before Truc could finish swallowing his first sip of coffee. Truc's sweetened black coffee gave his senses a rush of satisfaction. This coffee was thick and earthy like his grandmother use to brew. When he was a little boy his grandmother always made him weaken the strength of the coffee with milk. This coffee was a meal. Susie lowered her nose to smell the spoon full of pie and said, "Mm, thank you Truc." The sight and smell of the oven browned custard resting in the golden flaky crust made him feel cozy, he felt safe, and he felt like he was back in the womb of his family. Before chewing, he pressed each piece of pie, with his tongue, to his palette to squeeze out the flavor. The early October mid afternoon sunlight that filtered through the thin curtains gave the old kitchen a feel of friendly warmth.

"So Truc why are you here?"

From quiet contentment to crackling tension in a matter of seconds, it was now time to reveal the nature of his visit. Truc had never visited Susie, so why now? Truc had rehearsed his mission over and over and now suddenly rivers of fear and doubt were rushing through his body. He coughed to clear his throat and turned to face Susie. "Susie I need you to talk to someone for me. I need you to talk to Johnny."

A bewildered look spread across Susie's face, "Who?"

In an impatient tone Truc snapped, "Johnnie, our cousin Johnnie, Shotgun Johnnie."

Licking her lips, Susie swallowed and in her monotone voice said, "Oh, our cousin."

Nervously drumming his nails on the tabletop Truc whined, "I could never speak to Johnnie. All I can remember from the last time I spoke to him was the cold meanness in his eyes. I had an overwhelming desire to get away and fast. Everyone knows that in a split second it can turn dangerous talking to Johnnie and I know for whatever reason you and Johnnie have remained friends." Truc was having doubts this was going to work when he noticed that Susie look like a lizard staring at something on his shoulder. Why those blank eyes were always faking you out; was she really intently looking at him. "Susie I need you to ask him something. I have a job that I think may interest him. I will pay him and you." Silence, no response just crazy eyes staring at his shoulder or maybe something on the wall behind him. Clasping his hands together and taking a deep breathe Truc said, "Well, Susie, are you interested? Do you want to hear more?"

Susie's eyes were still pointing in the wrong direction, her small tight mouth barely moved when she softly said, "Yes."

"I won't beat around the bush, I need Johnnie to, I need him to kill someone." No reaction, her crazily aimed eyes never moved, she didn't speak, she didn't blink, and she didn't even swallow. Was she even looking at him? Taking another deep breath Truck said, "I can, I'm prepared to pay Johnnie thirty-five thousand dollars and another five thousand for you. Of course it will all be cash. Seventeen thousand five hundred for Johnnie and twenty five hundred for you when he accepts the job and the rest when the job is complete." Truc could feel a building urge to scream, he thought, "Is she alive; look at me you crazy bitch."

Then finally some movement, Susie slowly stood up and said, "More coffee?"

Truc feeling a trickle of sweat tracing his hairline and then racing down his jawbone was barely able to say between his rapid breaths of air, "Yes." Susie turtled her way to the stove but her eyes were eerily staring at Truc and before she could finish pouring coffee Truc loudly blurted out, "Say something."

She slow motion sat into her kitchen chair, the eyes again leveled at Truc's shoulder, then in her routine monotone voice Susie said, "Is this something that has to be done right away?"

Surprised by the business-as-usual type of question, Truc stuttered, "No not, not right away, but soon."

"Our cousin makes a run to Houston, the second week of each month, so he won't be home for a few more days and he never wants to be bothered for about four or five days after his Houston trip," Susie served herself another piece of pie. "So I couldn't talk to him until the end of next week." Her crazy eyes closed in satisfaction each time she took a bite of the custard pie.

Truc tried to steady his voice when he said, "Houston. What's in Houston?"

Susie sated with pie and with a calm contented look on her face said, "I don't know. He doesn't say and I don't ask."

Curious about his possible future employees Truc asked, "Do you and Johnnie socialize. Does he call you often?"

Her coffee cup almost to her thin lips stopped in mid tilt and as she leveled the cup, she softly said, "He calls me to say that he will come by to pick me up."

Swallowing the last of his second cup of coffee Truc asked, "What do you mean pick you up?"

"He knows I like Pastis and you can't find it anywhere around here and so he gets me a bottle in Houston and we spend an afternoon drinking the Pastis. I don't think he really likes the taste because he really dilutes his drink. I put half sparkling mineral water and half Pastis so that I don't get too tipsy. It's a beautiful drink, it makes me feel peaceful."

Amazed by the sudden profusion of words from Susie; Truc was intrigued by this relationship, "So you and Shotgun do this often?"

Susie's forehead furrowed up in a sign of confusion and said, "Who?"

Truc quickly and brusquely said, "Johnnie."

Susie shook her head, "No, no I only see Johnnie when he calls. We drink Patis, he cooks me dinner, we watch a movie and then he makes me a bed on the floor near the fireplace. Sometimes his girlfriend comes over and spends the night and sometimes she doesn't. In the morning he cooks me the best breakfast. Many years ago I went with Father to bring my brother, Lloyd to college. We stopped at a Holiday Inn for breakfast. I always thought that no one could fix a better breakfast until I tasted my favorite cousin's breakfast. He calls it brunch, I call it delicious."

Truc suspiciously said, "So you won't speak to him next week unless he calls?"

"He'll call. You said soon. How soon; a week, two weeks, a month?"

"Soon; if he says yes how will you contact me?"

"I'll call."

Staring down at his empty coffee cup, Truc was excited about executing the first part of his plan, but unnerved by the business-like tone of the conversation. "Could you call from a pay phone? Phone records. We don't want anything traced." Truc wasn't sure if Susie was still following their conversation when she cut three small pieces of pie and called each dog to come get a treat from her. "You think you could use a pay phone."

Susie turned her head facing Truc, but the eyes were blankly staring forty five degrees from his face and with the boss dog's head in her lap she said, "There are no pay phones around here but I can ask in the library to use the phone to call someone to come and get me. When I say come and get me that will be the signal to come to my house that evening. Come early evening if you can."

"I just don't want the phone records to link us; because I will probably become an instant suspect."

"Well thank you for the tarte ala bouillie; I will contact you as soon as possible."

Slightly rattled and then relieved to be so abruptly dismissed, Truc sprang from his chair and turned to leave. The paintings hung on the wall behind him drew his attention. Very good, almost abstract paintings of cypress swamps and moon-lit oceans drew him to closer inspection. Truc turned to Susie and said, "These are very good paintings, very eye-catching."

Susie's thin grin cracked into a huge smile, "Painting is a big release for me and my primitive en plein air painting style seems to suit my nature. I'm no Renoir, but I use the natural light the way I see it. My butlers will see you to the door, just be sure to close the door so that they don't decide to take an evening stroll." As Truc took a step to leave, the two slacker dogs hemmed him in on one side while the boss dog guarded his flank with terrorizing zeal.

"Goodbye Susie."

"Goodbye Truc."

Eight Days Of Misery

Sitting at his kitchen table smoking a cigarette, a habit that he took up again in the last 8 days, Truc felt uncomfortable with his plan and the emotional strain of waiting was creating a mental pressure that he was having trouble controlling. He had been planning his project for almost two years and he now felt unfulfilled with a constant inner voice buzzing about his meeting with Susie. He felt like he'd gone to a fast food restaurant and had ordered, "One murder please." He kept repeating the phrase that he had heard all of his life; "Dreams are always a lot better or a lot worse than the real thing." His Dad, his Grandfather and Uncles had all used this phrase to explain unexpected disappointments. His plan, his dream was a lot better than the real thing. Everything in his life was usually planned down to the last detail and so was this plan, this dream. But the first part of his plan, the meeting with Susie, was flat. There had been no bargaining highs, and no shared fears. The meeting with Susie seemed so clinical, so routine, so unconspiratorial, and so incomplete. He kept blaming himself for not conducting a more thorough meeting, but he knew it was those eyes, those damn crazy eyes. Witch eyes that saw the world on Susie's canvass vastly different from straight eyed souls. Any phone ringing for the last eight days had been a near stroke-inducing event. Answering a phone had become a heart pounding sickening chore. Then the question about Johnny, Shotgun Johnny, still remained. What made him think that Johnnie would be interested in committing murder? Johnnie could set him up, call the police and earn good citizen points. Working with Johnnie might be like playing with fire and with a very good chance of getting burnt. Truc had thought a lot about Johnnie over the past eight days. Johnnie had been Mr. Everything. Homecoming king, star quarterback with offers of a scholarship from colleges all over the country and academically he was at the top of his class. But his greatest talent was for baseball. He had been a rarity, a home run hitting great fast ball pitcher. Professional teams wanted him as soon as he got his diploma. Truc had been twelve years old when Johnnie seemed on top of the world. Everyone loved Johnnie. Everyone wanted to be Johnnie's friend, fan or just in his golden sphere, including the young Truc. Truc had been at the state championship game when the innocent world that he loved had been halted, had been changed. Everyone in the family called it the Black Day or The Tragedy. Truc liked to call it the Day of Heavy Sadness. That day of destiny had started out perfect. Truc's Dad had gotten tickets for the two of them to the state championship game and Johnnie was the starting pitcher. Their seats were two rows right behind Uncle Maurice's seats. Uncle Maurice was Johnnie's dad and where ever he sat in the stadium was where all the action usually took place. It was an unspoken privilege to sit near Uncle Maurice during one of Johnnie's usual great performances. Uncle Maurice correctly took a lot of credit for his son's athletic abilities. As soon as his young son could walk he had tirelessly worked with him to hone his skills. Uncle Maurice always had one thing on his mind and that was Johnnie and how to improve his skills. Johnnie had become the perfect son, an achiever at everything and now he was the starting pitcher in the state championship. It quickly became a game of dueling pitchers. Johnnie had pitched a remarkable game and had scored his team's only run with a solo homerun. In the seventh inning the opposing team relieved their pitcher, but Johnnie who had been on fire continued to pitch through the eighth inning and into the ninth. The bottom of the ninth inning and the score was one to naught. Johnnie had to retire only three more batters and he would be the reigning god of our world. The first batter, zoned in on the first pitch hurdling to the strike zone, an explosion and silence from our side of the stadium, then a distant cheer as the ball sailed into the heavens and out of the ballpark. Johnnie was already not perfect, he suddenly looked tired. The second batter took a base when Johnnie's fast ball burned his flesh. Johnnie was tired after eight innings of nearly flawless pitching. The coach should have relieved him but was probably fearful of Uncle Maurice's wrath. The next batter got a double with a line drive to the corner of right field. With a runner advanced to third base and one on second base, Johnnie did the unthinkable and walked the fourth batter. Bases loaded with no outs in the bottom of the ninth inning and Johnnie was visibly tired but still trying his best. Fifth batter, first pitch and it was sent back to Johnnie like a cannonball. Johnnie knocked down the line drive and all he had to do was throw the ball to home plate, to get the forced out. In his exhausted confusion Johnnie took a few seconds too long to grab the ball and then pulled back the throw to first to instead try for the out at home plate. The throw was too late, game over: two to one. Johnnie stood their alone on the pitching mound, silence on one side and cheers on the other. No teammate, no coach went on the field to congratulate him on a near perfect game. Alone he walked back to the dugout and out of the deafening silence came a voice, "You stupid idiot. You're an embarrassment." Johnnie didn't have to look up in the stands he knew it was his Dad's voice. Right before entering the dugout he looked up and saw his idol standing there in condemnation. In that fleeting horrible moment, Truc saw the corners of his hero's eyes and mouth turn down into a mask of tragedy. Johnnie never recovered.

He went home, packed his bags and left. It's been rumored that he and his Dad have not spoken in the last fifteen years. His Mom, Aunt Lucy, a weak, gossipy woman either did not try or couldn't convince Uncle Maurice to repair the damage. Johnnie turned down all scholarships and soon afterwards started his slow descent from grace. Johnnie was good at everything he did and was always in the spotlight with fans. He became a celebrated outlaw with new fans. Then the all-American sunk into an emotional pleasing world of violence and his old fans ran for the sidelines. The nickname, Shotgun Johnnie, symbolized his darker life. It had something to do with his woman and another man. All Truc knew was what he had heard from others was that he had righted a wrong with a shotgun. After that incident, the name Shotgun Johnnie was whispered in awe or fear or in sorrow for a fallen hero. His festering anger turned a venerated young man into a dangerous creator of fear. Truc always ended his negative dreaming with the fear that Johnnie just might make a visit to his house demanding all of the money. Truc had a hard time motivating his heavy legs to move when he heard his phone ringing in the bedroom. He cursed the ringing phone because he knew it was one of the irritating Saturday morning robocalls. Before he could say hello, the caller, in a familiar monotone voice said, "Come get me." His anxious depressed mood disappeared and for a few paralyzing minutes he stood next to his bed with his phone to his ear and the dial tone buzzing his brain. He sat on the edge of the bed slowly breathing deeply, to clear his head and calm his internal trembling. He had to get control of his emotions so that the next phase of his plan could have a positive outcome. Truc masked his feelings of panic with a calm subdued façade and started to think.

Why?

The waiting was over. "What You Looking At" Susie, had come through. Truc kept checking to see if he had brought everything, the boxes money, the sweets for Susie and paper and pen to write any notes about anything he needed to remember. The money was the most important thing that was needed for this meeting. For two years Truc had meticulously and routinely stored small sums of money for this day. He was always surprised when he opened the cash filled trunk to see the bulk that forty thousand dollars, mostly in twenties, created.

Truc knocked on the door and the greeters raced to the door with a chorus of yelps and growls, some fake and some vicious. Truc could see Susie through the dilapidated old curtains as she inched her way to the door. He could already feel an aggravation creep into his emotions because of Susie's slow crawl. Before she opened the door she said something that put an abrupt halt to the barking and growling. The door slowly creaked open, Susie's head popped into the small opening and said, "Well hello cousin, come on in." Truc squeezed through the small opening and was greeted by the boss dog silently baring his teeth while the two slacker dogs excitedly watched in anticipation. Susie already trudging toward the kitchen said, "Let's have some coffee." As Truc walked into the kitchen Susie pointed to the familiar chair and said, "Sit there."

Truc rested his three boxes on the kitchen table and handed the top box to Susie, "Here are some sweets for you."

Susie in quick-step mode grasped the box and opened it with the speed of a ravenous orphan. Looking into the magic box Susie's plain face began to glow and as she reached in she raved, "Mmm... thank you Truc, I love creamy pecan pralines." She bit into a praline, closed her eyes and said, "Creamy, small pieces of plump fresh pecans, not oversweet, perfect. Just like Aunt Vivian use to make. Let me fix us some coffee." Working quickly, Susie served each a cup of coffee and slid the box toward Truc and said, "Take one." In silence the two cousins ate creamy pralines and drank fresh drip-pot coffee. The three dogs were on high alert waiting to snatch up any crumbs dropped to the floor.

After eating his second praline Truc broke the silence, "So what did Johnnie have to say?"

Susie woke from her sweet addiction, scrunched up her upper lip and nose and said, "Who?"

Truc, an incredulous look on his face slowly and firmly said, "Our cousin Johnnie."

Aroused from her sugar euphoria Susie said, "Oh yes, our cousin, our cousin Johnnie. Yes, he cooked me the best breakfast."

Not sure if Susie was showing honest ignorance or playing a mean dull game, Truc said, "Well what did he say. What did Johnnie have to say about my offer?"

Shaking her head and chewing on her fourth praline Susie said with her lips coated in crumbs, "Yes he is very interested. He wants to know the person's name and why you want him killed."

Truc's suspicious mind warned of a set up. Was he being taped and set up for blackmail? "I can give him the name and his address that should be sufficient."

Susie licked her lips, drained the last of her coffee, and with a look of contentment faced Truc with her crazy eyes careening into space said, "He says he needs the name and the why so that he knows how he will do the job. He will protect your identity. He will protect you. Don't worry our cousin won't do you any harm." Susie's innocent conviction made it easier for the first time in two years to tell his story, hesitantly at first and then in a flood of relief.

Truc leaned towards Susie and in sotto voce whispered, "Benjamin Walrus. I want Ben Walrus killed." He looked at Susie and saw in her tabula rasa face his confessor. Susie's face expressed no emotions; her eyes seemed to be focused elsewhere and did not search his face for guilt. He could feel the emotional dam of inhibitions and guilt give way and he finally wanted to tell his story.

"I was a junior in high school when he arrived on campus. Long sandy hair, eyes light blue like a robin's egg, ultra white perfect teeth, athletic build, and a friendly laid-back sunny California personality. He turned heads wherever he walked. Students, teachers, coaches and administrators, both male and female were hypnotized by his presence. Parents were mesmerized by his attractive smile and easy-to-like personality. He easily became a member of the elite social strata of the high school class system. He was welcomed everywhere he went. He was the rock star of our high school. With movie star good looks he had his pick of the best looking girls our school could provide. He probably could have had a couple of the female teachers and a few mothers. We both played sports and so I got to know him on the fields of competition. We all worked hard, lifted tons of weights, to develop our skinny concentration-camp looking bodies. He swam in his family's pool to keep his perfect tan and his God-given physique. He looked like a surfer Tarzan. You couldn't help but see him as celestial. We were all envious, but would never have done anything or said anything to offend the super star. We would have been frowned upon by his admirers if any of my caste had displeased the celebrated superstar. It didn't take long for a few of us to see that there was a dark side to this person standing in the soft glow of his spotlight. He was and still is a manipulator of everyone; especially women. He loved intimate betrayal; it was his specialty. He would target a couple and seduce the girl. When the boyfriend found out, instead of beating Ben Walrus, he was maneuvered into thinking that a favor had been done. His girlfriend was a cheater and now he knew. He was a twister of facts with a razor sharp mind for evil. The devil serpent didn't just target couples; he took a delight in screwing up things between best friends. He was a loup-garou; a friend one minute and a predatory wolf the next. He had social teflon; nothing stuck to him, his sins, his misdeeds were always quickly forgiven and forgotten. Most mortals would take a life-time to pay for a sin or two; his wickedness would be forgiven before the sun could rise. Fortunately for me and my small group of friends we were very low on his radar. But even people in the lowest social strata could fall victim to his intimate destructive behavior; so he became our bête noir. By the end of the school year the California scourge had withered many human relationships. When he graduated, my friends and I thought we would never have to encounter this human plague again. We had heard that his summer job before going to college was as a stripper for women's parties and even a male stripper at a gay bar. He always liked showing his naked body. In the locker room he was always naked or just clothed in his brightly colored bikini underwear. There was a perversion in his need for people to glance at his naked ass."

Truc turned to see if his confessor was showing any signs of interest in his story. He couldn't tell if she was even paying attention or just thinking about another praline. To arouse some reaction from Susie, Truc said, "Could I have another cup of coffee."

Robotically, Susie stood up and stuttered at first, then said in a clear ringing tone, "So you want this Ben Walrus killed because he caused havoc in your high school."

Truc sneered and in an angry voice shouted, "Hell no Susie, he destroyed my marriage."

With no trace of emotions on her blank face, Susie slowly and carefully poured coffee into Truc's cup. "Oh yeah, you were married to Vivi Leblanc. She was a pretty bride; I saw pictures of your wedding."

Looking down at his cup of coffee, Truc's voice snarled and dripped in anger, "She worked at an advertising agency. If I had known that Ben Walrus owned the agency I would have never let her work there. I didn't realize that he still lived in town. He seduced her, they had a brief affair. She left me for what she thought was going to be a new life with her lover. She quickly found out that he was only interested in the chase and conquest and of course his ultimate pleasure—the destruction of a relationship. When she left she asked that I accept the fact that she was leaving and not create a huge ugly commotion. She said she wanted to remember me as a wonderful person that wanted her to be happy. She said that she loved Ben Walrus and she hoped that I would want to see her happy and not have a childish hatred of her. I became dizzy, faint and thought I was having a heart attack. It wasn't a heart attack, it was just a broken heart. It was the first big cut to my heart, not fatal, but the biggest physical hurt that I'd ever felt. My mind raced at a dizzy speed and my emotions tried to keep up. One minute I had a dark hatred for her and the next second I already felt lost without her. She had been my best friend; a relationship that would last until old age. She knew all my secrets. I told her things that I had never told anyone else. I felt embarrassed that such a traitor knew so much about me. Did she ever love me? Then the feeling of humiliation crammed its way into my destroyed self-esteem. I was a failure. How was I going to explain this to my family and friends? Was I a horrible lover? Was I boring? Why would she leave me for an awful person like Benjamin Walrus? How could she want to be with such a deceitful destroyer? Did I really know

Vivi? Was she like Ben Walrus? I wanted revenge, but if I had hurt him in any way I would still be in jail. This is my plan for revenge."

Susie with her forearm resting on the table and her eyes pointing in an absurd angle leaned towards Truc and in a soft barely audible tone said, "What about Vivi?"

Searching Susie's face for any clue to her thoughts he spoke to her directionally challenged eyes, "No, I believe that she fell under the influence of this sorcerer's magical spells. I've seen it before. " Chewing the inside of his lower lip he looked away, "Susie I had a dream of a large happy family. Lord Warlock, Mr. California shattered that dream and I can't move on until he has tasted my revenge. Susie he destroyed my dream. He destroyed my dream. Do you have any dreams?"

Susie nibbling on another praline and not realizing that Truc wasn't really interested in her dreams, "Have you ever seen those ancient Greek vases that are in museums? One has a person staring straight ahead, a feminine eye with what looks like eyeliner at each canthus. Levantine eyes. There is a reporter for the New York Times and every time I see him on T.V. I see the eyes that I dream about. But mostly I just dream about what it must be like in heaven. Do you believe in heaven?"

Astonished by the sudden and unexpected revelations Truc sank deeper into his chair and let out his pent up breath, "I'm a doubter."

With a sugary lower lip, Susie's voice got louder, "I feel safest when I am with a doubter. I'm wary of people that have total conviction, unbending faith in their belief that there is or isn't a heaven, a god."

Not wanting to debate religion, Truc got back to business. "Well here is the money. The small box is for you, the larger one is for Johnnie and the envelope contains a picture of Ben Walrus and his work and home address. I also included the name of the gym where he is a member and a nightclub that he frequents. Do you have any idea when he'll execute the plan? I'd like to know about when it will happen so that I can have people around me to verify my alibi."

Susie took another praline and broke it into three pieces to share with her pack of professional beggars. "He said it would be about four weeks before it can happen. He has his monthly trip to Houston. Then he has to do reconnaissance to come up with his plan and something to do with cooler weather and fog."

Irritated that it would take so long, he snapped, "Houston trip! I bet Shotgun Johnnie is making his monthly drug run."

Susie furrowed her brow in confusion and said, "Who?"

Annoyed, Truc roughly questioned, "Why do you always look confused when I say Johnnie's name."

Sweeping praline crumbs from the table top to the floor created a scramble by the four legged floor cleaners. "That's not our cousin's name. Uncle Maurice didn't think his birth name was a good name for a sports star; so he starting calling him Johnnie. My Mum and Grandma always called him by his birth name-Wayne Joseph.

With a snicker, Truc asked, "So the superstar, the outlaw, his name is Wayne?"

Tiring of her visitor, Susie sighed, "I usually just call him cousin. Any way, he said that it would probably happen on a workday during the morning rush hour. Watch for the newspaper headlines so that you know that the job has been done and then I will contact you that evening. The final payment will be at that meeting."

Hesitant to end the meeting, Truc held up four fingers, "About four weeks...workdays...morning rush hour... bring money. Anything else I need to know?"

Susie slowly stood to end the conversation, said, "I think that's it. Just close the door behind you so my pups don't roam the streets tonight."

Surprised at how weak his legs felt when he stood up he said, "O.K. Susie I'll see you in four weeks." As he stiffly walked to the door, the boss dog escorted him bumping his leg a number of times to show who was in charge. The slacker dogs wrestle with each other as they watched his other flank.

The Long Wait

Truc started going to work thirty minutes early so that he could have an alibi. For two weeks he felt like he was going to bust out of his skin because of all the tension and anticipation. His plan was about to come to fruition. Hopefully everything went smoothly; but if it went horribly wrong it didn't matter as long as Ben Walrus was killed. By the third week he was tired, irritable and ready for it all to be over. His mind and body had been working overtime and the adrenaline had fried his energy reserves. By the third week he was exhausted but dared not take a day off of work to recharge his body. For three weeks he had kept replaying the meeting with Susie. He kept hearing her voice come alive when she told him of her unfulfilled dream of normal eyes and how she settled for her version of a dream of heaven. Then there was the surprise that his boyhood idol, Johnnie, was not Johnnie; he was Wayne. What other family secrets he didn't know about. When the thoughts of the meeting were not racing through his mind he was contemplating the last minutes of Ben Walrus's life or thinking of ViVi. How could he let her know that this vengeance was for the both of them? He couldn't sleep because his mind would never shut down. He couldn't eat because his stomach was in constant turmoil. He hadn't spoken to Vivi in almost two years and now he wanted to sit across from her and tell her that he understood. Many times he'd seen the evil work of Ben Walrus. He had seen the devastation that this man could create. In making such a life changing decision he needed a companion, a friend to listen to his thoughts, his fears. She had been the only person he could spend hours with in conversation. He felt like he needed her more than ever.

On an early November morning, four weeks since his last meeting with Susie, Truc opened his backdoor to leave for work and was confronted with a fog so thick he couldn't see his car parked twenty feet away in his driveway. Already aggravated because he hadn't slept most of the night and now he had to drive in impenetrable fog. He would rather drive in a rainstorm, than in this thick fog. Truc loved the cool weather that created the autumn fog but always feared driving in it.

At ten pass eight o'clock Truc could see from his office that many of the secretaries and a few administrators were still in the reception area discussing something. Five minutes later he could see that the group in the reception area had not broken their huddle and everyone had a somber expression. He couldn't help himself, he had to go and find out about the gossip. He walked up to the group and said, "Is something wrong?"

Fat Bill was the first to speak, "I thought I would be late for work because of the fog and all the police in my neighborhood. Jackie who lives in my neighborhood said that her husband just called and said that he just spoke to a policeman that told him there had been a gruesome murder in the neighborhood."

Truc's legs became wobbly weak and he felt a panicky urge for a bowel movement when he heard the news. As he turned to seek refuge in his office he barely got out the words, "Who was it?"

Mean Ms. Mildred, the office shrew with the orange red hair, who knew everyone's personal life or thought she did said, "We don't know, but I'm going to make a few phone calls."

When he reached the comfort of his desk, the barrier to the outside world, his mind and body was reeling from the avalanche of adrenaline burning through his semi paralyzed body. He could barely swallow because his rapidly beating heart was taking up too much space in his chest and throat. The long wait was over; he knew Ben Walrus lived in Fat Bill and Jackie's neighborhood. They said it was a gruesome murder. What did they mean by gruesome; weren't all murders gruesome? He started doing breathing exercises to calm his body and mind. He knew that if his colleagues saw this physical reaction that it would arouse suspicions. When the breathing exercises started their calming effects and he could have rational thought he was surprised by his reaction. He thought when he'd get the good news that his plan had been completed he would have felt a weight being lifted from his heart; instead it had been trembling fear. As his fear subsided and his confidence grew he was embarrassed by his weakness and convinced himself that he had done the world a favor. He would busy himself with work and at lunch he'd leave to buy a newspaper so that he could read about this morning's event.

The Lunch of Turmoil

Truc stayed in constant motion, because of the adrenaline fueled energy he worked nonstop all morning in his office but accomplished very little. He decided to take an early lunch at eleven, his mission was not food, but newspaper headlines. He didn't want to seem in a hurry so he took his time getting to the elevator engaging in small talk with the secretaries. He was glad that no one, not even heavily rouged Mean Mildred, mentioned the big event that had occurred that morning. He was ten feet from the elevator when he heard Rita's voice, "Truc could I join you for lunch?" Truc winced and turned to face Rita, the assistant manager of sales. He could feel the warmth that her voluptuous body always radiated. A five foot tall brunette, very curvy almost borderline pudgy with a freckled cherubic inviting smile and a tendency to wear clingy clothes that captured hungry eyes from all her male colleagues.

"Sure, I'm only going to the Venetian to get a sandwich; but you're very welcome to join me." Rita wasn't part of his plan, but he couldn't think of an excuse and maybe she had news about the murder. The drive to the Venetian was filled with small talk chatter that irritated Truc and Rita never mentioned this morning's big event. Once they were seated, Truc realized that he wasn't hungry and he could feel the discomfort of heartburn.

Larry, the owner of the Venetian, walked up and smiled, "I'm short on help today. What can I get yawl?"

Rita, in her sexy hoarse voice, said, "I'll take your lunch special and a glass of water."

Hoping that Rita would only get something to drink; Truc quickly scanned the menu and said, "Just give me a BLT and a coke." The small talk continued until the food arrived, the moment Truc always dreaded when eating a meal with Rita. Rita was always a symphony of mouth sounds at mealtime. She was a slurper, a cruncher, an open mouth chewer and would suck food off of a spoon with gusto. She couldn't drink a glass of water without gulping and gurgling. Every crunch, every gurgle, every sight of teeth chomping and churning green and yellow food tighten the muscles in the back of his neck. By the end of the choral feast Truc's neck muscles were so taut he could barely turn his head. When he reached the safety of his office, his head was throbbing and his stomach was a tornado of acid. He closed his office door, dimmed the lights, laid reports on his desk, sat in his chair, elbows on the desktop, head in hands, closed his eyes and focused his mind on Vivi.

Headlines

Truc unlocked the door and stepped inside his cool dark oasis. His house, dusty but neat, was his shelter, his haven from the world. His refuge was not sparkling clean, not by a long shot, but it was neat and orderly. His major housekeeping skill was that everything had a place so everything should be in its place. He knew he was almost neurotic in finding the perfect spot for his household items and treasures. It was his form of mental feng shui. Walking into his audio room, he threw the newspaper on the couch and started undressing. He could already feel some if his stress ease away now that he felt a relief from social confinement and was in the comfortable safety of his home. He had read the headlines of the newspaper, but planned on reading the whole article as soon as he could calm down and have rational thoughts. His stomach was still having quiver spasms and his muscles ached from being so tense for most of the day. Dressed only in his briefs, Truc bent over to touch his toes to stretch tight back muscles then suddenly the phone rang. Neuron electro chemical impulses bolted from his temples and surged down his spine and exploded in his lower gut. He hovered over the phone, letting it ring two more times before he quickly brought it to his ear and yelled, "Hello."

The familiar slow monotone response was: "come and get me tomorrow at four o'clock".

With the dial tone ringing in his ear, Truc repeated over and over four o'clock. The phone still to his ear he walked over to his small bar and poured a jigger of Jameson. Truc held the whiskey in his mouth for a second before slowly swallowing the smooth fire. By the time the fire reached his stomach the numbness was already spreading. After drinking his second jigger of Jameson, he sat on his couch with a faraway stare and wished he had someone to talk to, to release his emotions. He had only been able to verbally work through his problems and release his inner turmoil with one person, Vivi. He tried to hate her, he tried to get her out of his mind, but he couldn't, he missed her. He missed having a friend. He wished there was a way that he could let her know that the relationship killer, that had destroyed their lives, had paid for it with his life. He noticed the newspaper and slowly unfolded it to the front page. On the middle top of the front page was a picture of the smiling Ben Walrus. Most people would rank second or third page. Just below his smiling picture was the headline in bold print—**Shocking Homicide**. He took a deep breath then read about his completed project.

Early this foggy Friday morning, prominent businessman Ben Walrus, was murdered on his front lawn. Police believe the grisly crime occurred at around seven this morning. Claretta Petacci, the victim's wife discovered her husband's mutilated body and called 911. Authorities have said that the victim had been hacked numerous times, almost decapitated and died at the crime scene. Benjamin Walrus, a prominent businessman and civic leader was married with two children. A native of Golden Ville, California; Mr. Walrus was an active citizen involved in many civic organizations in the community. Police believe, due to this morning's extremely thick fog there were no witnesses to the gruesome crime. People in the neighborhood did report seeing a tall black male with a small Afro haircut wearing a knee length trench coat and carrying a knapsack. Authorities are asking that anyone with any information to call 988-888-8181.

Mutilated, hacked, decapitated, what the hell was Johnnie, Shotgun Johnnie thinking? Truc could feel a slow creeping, black dread enveloping his thoughts. Did Johnnie get high on his Houston drugs and go to a killing festival? All this blood and gore was not necessary; just a bullet to the head would have been sufficient and clean. Truc was beginning to think Johnnie may not have been the right choice for his plan. What was to stop Johnnie's killing spree? What if Johnnie wanted all of the money and no one to implicate him? Truc brought the bottle of Jameson to the couch and had another jigger of whiskey. Looking inwardly at his dark thoughts, Truc tried to envision hacked, mutilated, and decapitated. After hours of relentless streaming thoughts and three quarters of a bottle of Jameson he could hear the birds outside his window begin their morning songs. Before dosing off, whiskey and negative thoughts had increased his fear of Shotgun Johnnie.

The Last Meeting

Truc turned the doorknob of the front door to leave, and then stopped to recheck that he had everything he needed. He checked his pockets and looked around and went over his mental checklist keys, gloves, two boxes of money, wallet, pistol and hooded jacket. Truc slowly opened the door and the cold damp breeze tightened his face. The cold front had come in yesterday and was making itself known. The late afternoon dark winter sky was a water coloring of gray fading into black smudges that covered the whole vaulted inner dome. He thought if it would only be drizzling it would be a perfect day to laze at home and totally relax and rejuvenate. He welcomed an occasional dark day like today to sit and think, to contemplate, to daydream. He had just one stop, to get sweets for Susie, before going to his last meeting with her. He hoped this would be the last time he had to deal with "What You Looking At" Susie.

Truc knocked on the door, he could see through the dilapidated curtains the usual greeters giving a slap stick performance racing, sliding and tumbling to the door. They seemed unusually excited with their barking and yelping to an extreme. Susie came into focus and looked different, when she opened the door he could see that she had dressed for the occasion. She was wearing a long billowy dark green cotton skirt that was pleated at the waist, a golden yellow loose fitting blouse and what looked like a faded orange Juliet cap perched in her teased golden hair. As usual she made a small opening and said "Come in cousin."

Truc squeezed through the small opening and handed Susie a white box, "Here you go Susie I bought you some sweets." The enlightened furry greeters knew that Truc plus a box meant a treat and their eyes instantly became transfixed on the box. The hypnotized dogs followed the box like robotic cult worshippers.

Susie closed her eyes and brought the box to her nose so that she could smell the aroma of her sweet surprise. Slowly gliding to the kitchen, with her minions dancing in delight she said, "Thanks Truc, let's go into the kitchen."

Truc stepped through the kitchen door and saw Johnnie. The surprise constricted his neck muscles enough to open his mouth into silent shock. The warm oven- heated kitchen air became a cauldron of tension. He could feel the air vibrate with a background thrum of danger.

Johnnie stood up and offered his hand, "Hello Truc, it's good to see you."

Truc offered his hand and with his maw agape stiffly walked to his previously assigned chair. A heavy sigh of burden drifted from his mouth as he placed the two boxes on the table. He sat, looked at Johnnie and could feel the high pitched metallic words clang out of his mouth. "This is a surprise."

Johnnie sat comfortably with military posture, square shouldered, thick neck, Indian black hair, piercing blue eyes and the smile, the familiar welcoming smile that always inspired trust. Johnnie started to speak but a shout of childish gaiety interrupted, "Yes beignets. Oh Truc you always bring my favorite treats." Looking down at her powdered treasures her face was hidden by the box lid. When her eyes rose over the box lid they were staring straight at Truc. The warm electric air instantly switched to a dizzy surreal nightmarish chill. "What You Looking At" Susie was staring with intense unwavering, unblinking eyes. Beautiful hazel eyes rimmed in dark to fading green, heavy eyeliner in each corner, high cheekbones and puffy bare lips made "What You looking At" Susie excitingly beautiful. No one had ever looked at her eyes; her directionally challenged eyesight had been such an aggravation, so repulsive that most people just ignored her. Her eyes had blinded everyone to her beauty.

Unable to break her hypnotic stare, he could hear Johnnie laughing, "It's going to take her some time to get use to her new directional focus."

Susie stood up and a sexy petite smile surrounded her lips, "Three cups of coffee coming right up." Both men appraised Susie's newly found beauty as she walked to the stove to get the drip pot coffee.

Johnnie realizing he was wolfishly eyeing his cousin, turned to Truc and said, "I just wanted to let you know the details of the service I provided."

Susie poured each a cup of coffee, opened her treasure box, "Who wants a beignet?" Susie's petite smile exploded ear to ear when both men declined a beignet.

Truc's gloved hand slowly brought the cup of steaming coffee to his lips. He was able to slow his racing thoughts and heartbeat long enough to realize that this frightening meeting might actually be a golden opportunity.

Focusing on Truc, Johnnie said, "I wanted you to know what you paid for. I would have done the job sooner but if you don't feed hungry antique dealers on a regular basis they quickly shift their loyalties."

Truc crinkled his brow in confusion, said, "Antiques?"

Beaming his seductive smile, Johnnie laughed, "Maurice is the buyer. He concentrates on rural central and northern Louisiana. There are treasures unique to this area."

Truc put his hands up to stop Johnnie, "Maurice your Dad. I thought you were estranged?"

Johnnie looking down at his hands, "We were for a long time and for a while I was comfortable with violence and chaos. I lived a hedonist life style and each night loved a fille de joie. Maurice and Lucy, like most parents, have that ability to add a vinegar to their child's life that causes guilt to flare. Nothing that exists is forever and that includes emotions. Plus I didn't want to become another Biff Loman. That would have been so easy. I was angry for a long time; but anger is the biggest killer. A killer of dreams, people, relationships, countries and the list can go on forever. Living with anger is like swimming every day in the Devil's comfortable lake. So Maurice and I set up a partnership. It's a very profitable partnership. He gives a good price for the antiques that he buys and I transport the treasures to Houston and sell them for a fair price. Buyers from San Antonio, Austin, Dallas, Oklahoma and as far as Denver converge on Houston each month and expect something special from me."

Truc inwardly smiled and thought Johnnie the little old antiques dealer was probably losing his edge. He turned to see Susie's contented face chewing on a beignet. The sugary white powder on her jaw line added to her ethereal beauty. Johnnie's smile disappeared and his eyebrows flared upward at the ends and his eyes took on the cold gaze of a raptor. His words were steady and serious. "I already knew about Ben Walrus. Hundreds of people would have loved to kill him. The world is better with his death. I watched and studied his early morning routine and I knew about when he would leave for work in the morning. He would leave a little early so that he could have coffee and sweets at his secretary's house before both departed in separate cars to go to work. I knew that there might be a good chance for fog. The gods really smiled on us that morning because the cool front that came in that night came dressed the next morning in the thickest furriest gray fog. Someone standing ten feet away would not have seen Ben Walrus scurry crablike to hell. My disguise was a short tight Afro wig and some cocoa colored face paint. I looked ridiculous, but it did give me some cover. I parked my motorcycle in a grocery store parking lot and walked three blocks to his house. When I arrived at his house and under the cover of fog and darkness I walked onto his front lawn blended in with the trunk of his massive mossy oak tree and waited. When I saw him walk out of his front door, I rapidly walked to his car and waited to emerge from the fog when he grabbed the handle of his new small fog-wet black sports car."

Truc had to break the tense suffocating grip Johnnie had on his soul. He turned and saw Susie looking at her image reflected on the side of the shiny old toaster. He lifted a finger and said, "Susie could I have another cup of coffee?" He knew he had to listen to the whole story before he made his decision.

Susie's trance broken, jumped up and said, "Sure Mr. Dessert Man."

Johnnie with his serious arched eyebrows never took his focus off of Truc. He said in a rough command, "Get me a beer."

Johnnie waited for Truc's eyes to reposition on him and continued the report. "The beast was surprised when I emerged from the fog. Politely, but definitely in a condescending harsh sneer he said, "Can I help you?"

One hand in my trench coat pocket and the other concealed behind my back I said, "Do you remember Truc and his ex-wife, Vivi?"

The bully, the destroyer of dreams, took his hand off of the car door handle turned to face me and in a threating manner said, "What the hell do you want?"

Johnnie deliberately building the tension slowed his speech, "You do remember Truc, don't you? Well he paid me to kill you and with that I swung the hand ax that I had been concealing behind my back. So I'd presume his last thoughts before falling into the infinite darkness and meeting the Angel of Death were of you. The ax sliced into the neck where it meets the shoulder. It happened so quickly he didn't even have time to flinch. His eyes spotted the ax as it came down. He stayed upright as the blood spewed out of his neck like a fountain of claret. I hadn't planned on the intense anger I had for this man and I stuck him a second time on the top front of his head. I didn't expect the face to split as it did. I immediately thought, it will definitely be a closed casket. His body fell back and he landed in a muted thud. Blood and brains were everywhere. As I turned to leave I swung the ax between his spread eagle legs. I had one last insult for this devil spawn. The ax stuck in bone; so I had to brace my foot on his stomach to yank the ax out of his body. Minty aftershave, iron scented blood and now shit all mingled to provide, a repulsive aroma. Mr. Walrus was creating steam in the cool morning air. Before I walked out of his yard I put the bloody ax and gloves in my knapsack. A few people saw from their car a tall black man with an Afro haircut, wearing a knee length trench coat and carrying a knapsack. When I reached my motorcycle, which was still cloaked in heavy fog, I removed the trench coat and put it in the sack. When I had driven a few blocks I removed the wig. When I arrived at my home everything, the wig, the trench coat, the shoes, the sack, all clothes and the face paint was burned in my backyard fire pit. The motorcycle has been cleaned numerous times and the hand ax is covered in mud at the bottom of Bayou Lafourche. Mr. Ben Walrus is now taking that eternal walk in the Valley of Death. I just hope his temporary guide is not Mignon. Mission accomplished." Johnnie went silent, his hands laying palm down on the table and his serious stare was still focused on Truc.

Truc knew it was his turn to talk or act. He knew he would never have a better opportunity to complete his plan. Truc suddenly stood up and at the same time pulled the pistol from his pocket and fired the bullet into Johnnie's forehead. In one quick motion he leveled the gun sight with Susie's face and pulled the trigger. The blast knocked her out of the chair onto the kitchen floor. Truc's ears were ringing from the sound of the gunshots, but he could hear the frightened yelps of the boss dog and could see the panic in his actions. Truc leveled the gun to shoot the dog then lowered it and said with a malicious sneer, "I won't waste a bullet; I'll let the dog catcher gas your flea bag ass." Truc put the warm gun back into his coat pocket, picked up the two boxes of money and the empty box of beignets, looked at Shotgun Johnnie and said, "No witnesses and at half price." When Truc left through the front door he didn't completely close it and as he drove off in Rita's car the two slacker dogs went tumbling down the front steps and ran off into the darkness.

In the house Johnnie was still seated in the kitchen chair with his head tilted backwards; his eyes seemed to be looking at the hole in his head. On the floor, "What You Looking At" Susie was struggling to crawl to the phone. The boss dog with crying yelps nudged Susie, trying to encourage his friend.

Vivi

Quick stepping in high heels she made the sound of a rapid steady tap of a snare drum. She could be heard before she came rushing into the reception area of her office. She was tired of the detectives coming to question her about the murder of Ben Walrus, that piece of trash. She had angrily told the detective to leave her alone and to focus his investigation on the hundreds of people who would have loved to kill the bastard. When she entered the reception area her secretary could see that Vivi's anger was boiling. Timidly the young secretary said, "You must have made someone very happy because huge bouquets of flowers were just delivered for you."

Vivi slowly and cautiously entered her office and saw two huge bouquets of flowers on her desk. Anyone that really knew her knew that she hated flowers from a florist. The smell always reminded her of when she was a little girl and she had smelled the flowers at her mother's funeral. The two towering bouquets of red, green, blue and orange had already given her office the smell that she associated with death. Vivi pulled the card from one of the bouquets and when she read it she fell to her knees crying. The card had no signature, just four words.

10/08/2011

THE PANTY MAN

He really liked his new job working in the warehouse, but he tended to get so busy that he often missed his thirty minutes for lunch. He was disappointed with his new uniform; it was too red and much too big. He was surprised that they had written his nickname, Stick, on his name placket and of course the number 999. As he quickly walked down the hall he was hoping that the cafeteria was still open, because he was starving and he knew he was too skinny to continually miss meals. When he turned the corner, he was happy to see that the cafeteria lights were still on.

As he burst through the cafeteria doors, he saw Deputy Aaron, the cafeteria guard, wrinkle his nose and held up his hands in a questioning gesture. Portraying an innocent look and throwing his hands in the air he said, "They said I could come and eat." Keeping it vague and using no names just in case he was breaking any of the million rules.

When he reached for his tray he saw that his favorite cook, stupid Junius Head, was still working. Junius was working here because of his habitual sin of bigamy. Stupid Junius married seven times and never got a divorce, thinking he would not have to pay alimony if he didn't ever divorce any of his wives. He thought it would be better, to be thought of as a dead-beat, useless, and noncontributing husband, than to pay alimony.

"Hey man, I'm so glad to see you guys are still open," said Stick as he eyed his meal choices.

Stick could never decide if Junius was always happy and had a constant smile on his face or if his teeth were so big that his lips could never fully cover his teeth and gums. "Damn right, we can't close down until Deputy Aaron say we can go; asshole."

Licking his lips, Stick cried out, "Oh yes, give me some of that fried catfish. Is that fresh from our ponds?"

"Sho' is."

"Give me mostly fish and just a little bit of white beans with no rice."

His maximum smile still gripping his face, Junius shook his head and snapped at Stick, "No rice with your beans. No wonder your ass is so skinny."

Stick entered the dining area, glanced around and saw an empty just-used cafeteria. Deputy Aaron was to one side and at the far end of the cafeteria was the back of a solitary diner. Always looking for a friendly gab session, Stick's long skinny legs carried him to his new social encounter. When he got close to the unmoving back, he began to have second thoughts and then he saw Deputy Aaron slowly walk to this karma cloaking area of the cafeteria. Hesitantly, Stick faced the stranger and stammered, "Hello, I hate to eat alone. May I sit at your table?" The square-shouldered stranger looked up from his plate of uneaten catfish, suspiciously eyed Stick and motioned with his eyes for Stick to sit down. Stick quickly tabled his tray, stuck his hand out to the stranger and in his naïve manner said, "My name is Shady Boodo."

The stranger's beat up and weathered face cracked a smile. He raised his huge hand to gently shake Stick's hand and without offering a name he laughed, "Damn, your mom condemned you as soon as you were born."

Shady sat down and with an easy smile on his face started his chatter, "Most people call me, Stick."

Still grinning, the stranger said, "Oh I much rather Shady Boodo. It warns people of who they may be dealing with."

Stuffing a big piece of catfish into his mouth, Stick muttered, "Oh no, that's not me, if anything I am probably too honest. No, I'm in here for selling weed. I was selling too much and to the wrong people. I was so gullible."

The stranger's earthy brown eyes penetrated Stick's space, took a deep breath and said, "Boy I sure could use some good weed." Shady, lowering his voice so that Deputy Aaron couldn't hear him said, "I'll see what I can do for ya." Tears came to Shady's eyes when he tried to swallow two trips to the mouth. "Man, this is damn good catfish."

The stranger looked down at his uneaten catfish and said, "Yeah, it's usually pretty good."

When the stranger's eyes were diverted to his plate, Shady took a quick glance to study his table mate. Rugged, but peaceful looking with a handsome beat up face, the stranger was hard to attach an age to, maybe forty, maybe fifty. When the stranger looked up Shady quickly went to work on his white beans and as if talking to his plate said, "And what is your name, sir?"

When Shady looked up, the stranger's focused stare was almost paralyzing. After a moment of silent tension the stranger said, "You'd probably know me by the name Panty Man."

Shady closed his eyes to concentrate, then smiled and asked, "The bank robber? Panty Man the bank robber?"

A small satisfied smile spread across the stranger's face as he shook his head yes.

Shady guffawed, "I remember. You were all over T.V. Instead of a mask you used women's panties to disguise yourself." Shady slapped the table and choked out, "Why panties?" Tonguing his white beans to the side of his mouth so that he could repeat, "Why panties?"

The stranger still smiling said, "Well first of all they were not panties, they were my woman's big granny drawers. My head is kind of big and that's all she wore, it was just a natural fit. I never really liked wearing a mask; it really scares the tellers; so I usually wore a simple disguise. A mask is sometimes sinister. I figured when it was all over and the tellers told their story to their friends about being robbed they would get particular satisfaction when saying, "And that crazed robber was wearing underwear on his head, and then take a drink of their beer and have a good laugh with their friends. I could have been killed by a nut wearing drawers on his head."

Shady excitedly pushed his fork-cleaned plate to the side, so that he could focus on the stranger.

Remembering good times, the stranger's face creased at the eye corners and his mouth relaxed into a small grin. "I recorded all the shots from the security cameras that were shown on T.V. Sometimes we would have a laugh fest watching the DVD that I made. We would laugh until our throats were raw. I always looked like an idiot with an eye looking out of each leg hole and my nose looking like a covered erection." His face turned ruddy red and unsuccessfully stifled a laugh. "My favorite was the time I wore the panties decorated with large multicolored hearts. Even the teller had a hard time keeping a straight face."

Shady spied a small blue tattoo on the inside of the strangers left wrist. Was it a dog? No, it was a tattoo of a blue dragon with black eyes and a breath of red flames. "So that's why you're here."

The stranger furrowed his brow and became serious. "Oh no, the man could never catch me. I've robbed banks for thirty years. I was too good and never greedy. It was a great job, visit a few banks and move on to another place to explore. In the Midwest I used a plastic carrot nose for a disguise and so I was known as the Carrot Man. Different disguises, different silly T.V. names, I became a different character in various parts of this fine country and at various times in my life."

Swallowing the last of his tea, Shady wiped his mouth with his napkin, leaned forward and whispered, "After thirty years, how many banks have you robbed?"

The stranger looked down at the bright white table top to do his mental math and spoke to hands, "Let's see, usually 10 to 12 banks a year, times 30 years. I would estimate between 300 and 350 bank jobs. I've had my picture taken many times."

Shady slapped the super white table top and laughed loudly, "Man, you got a video history of your career. You could be a professor. Doctor of Banking. Dr. Panty Man."

Deputy Aaron uncomfortable with the loud talk passed by the white table and said, "O.K. guys we are already past our allotted time, ten minutes and we got to go."

The stranger smiled at Deputy Aaron and said, "Yes sir. Thanks Aaron."

He was so involved in this surprising and unexpected conversation, Shady barely noticed Deputy Aaron, "So why you in here?"

The stranger, shaking his head slowly from side to side said, "I had a really bad week."

Eager to hear more, Shady lamented, "Oh, come on man. A bad week?"

The stranger sat back into his chair and looked like a sage preparing for a life lesson, began to describe his week of darkness. "It started on a Monday I was driving to my yoga class when I was stopped and ticketed for not wearing a seatbelt. I always wear a seatbelt. I just forgot. I felt like I had bumped into a pickpocket with a uniform. Do you remember when you were young and your Mom held your hand when you crossed the street. Mommy is still by our side, but now she is wearing a uniform. When I finished working with my yogi master, I felt so at peace that I just sat by the window watching the rain lightly wash everything. The morning ticket could no longer hold on to my psyche. No one could ruin my day. I got into my reliable old Ford Taurus. I started her and turned on the wipers to clear the windshield of the lightly misting rain. I drove for about 300 feet and then there were suddenly police lights behind me. I got a ticket for using my windshield wipers without having the head-lights turned on. I suddenly wanted to kill the bastard, he had ruined my day. Determined not to let others control my emotions, I went for a jog Tuesday morning. When I got back home I showered, cooked breakfast for me and my beautiful woman and told her to stay at home and enjoy the lovely spring morning. I would go and do the grocery shopping. In the cradle of the protection of my seatbelt I drove to the grocery store. When I pulled into my parking area and turned off the radio I could hear a horn blowing and someone yelling. When I got out of the car I could see a red faced man hanging out the window of his black suburban yell-ing and waving his fist at me. When he saw my hesitation, my confusion, he gained bravura, held on to his outrage, and exited his vehicle as he slam the door shut. He rudely hurdled himself into my personal space; too close for my comfort, my safety. I won't repeat the curse words he used, but he said I had ogled his wife. His lips stretched into a cruel smile and in a deep growling voice he claimed that I had insulted him and his wife when I leered at his wife's body. Once again I was caught feasting my eyes on someone else's bounty. I've never been able to look away from a beautiful woman. I know sometimes it goes from a little peek to gawking with pornographic thoughts. The visual inspection, the feast, is never complete until I can peruse her backside. I can't help it, it's like an addiction, and my eyes become butt-magnetized. Any shape or color, as long as the delight has that little heated rise about it. If dazing at a great rump was a paid occupation; I'd ask for overtime every day. Butt-dreaming creates peace. My immature reasoning."

The stranger's eyes looked up as his lips spread into a grin of embarrassment. "Well back to the pepper head that wanted to kick my ass. He pointed his finger at the car and told me that I had better get my ass over to his car and apologize to his wife. Instead of taking the easy route in this silliness; I tempted fate by foolishly baiting an angry man. When I reached the passenger window I could see the offended wife had a sexy but demure smile. Her blouse and jeans were stretched tight over her curves. Tight jeans are the international code for: look at my ass. I should have given a quick short apology; but instead I rattled my phone number and told her to call me for a good time. Then I quickly moved into a fighter's stance waiting for the onslaught. His oversized lower mandible opened to spew out more curses and then he threatened to kill me. Next time he showers someone with his low class insults and threats, they may just shoot him. His twisted red face would have been perfect for a horror movie. Other customers that had stopped to see the show of bluff said that someone should call the police to have the cretin arrested. The enraged husband had a choice; show some action or walk away. He chose to continue his verbal assault as he backed away to the safety of his vehicle. Before his sweating greasy red face disappeared into his tank he let loose one more tirade of insults and threats. The screeching of tires, some more yelling, encased in his metal and plastic weapon, the pepper head sped out of the parking lot. I went home and meditated. I refused to allow a mean and ill equipped low-life to control my emotions."

Delighted to be sharing the dining table with such an interesting confederate, Shady leaned closer to the stranger and in a hushed voice said, "I understand your butt addiction; I'm a titty man."

The stranger smiled and grunted," That's because you still a momma's boy. You never broke away from the tit."

Shady's gentle laugh quietly echoed in the empty cafeteria. "I can't help it, my eyes are titty magnetized. That's just two days, what happened the rest of the bad week?"

The stranger shifted in his chair and continued his saga. "Wednesday morning we decided to go bike riding in this wonderful park. It was a beautiful cool sunny day. We were enjoying the peace, the serenity of this wonderful park, when suddenly this kid pulled alongside of me and demanded that we pull over. This polite prick informed us that we would each receive a citation for riding in the park without wearing helmets and that we had to walk our bikes out of the park. We went home and got drunk; we had to get our minds off of foolish rules. Thursday was a good day until the mail came. Our internet provider informed us that the special that we had signed up for was over last month and since we hadn't called to cancel they put us on their super deluxe combination and now we were locked in for the next twelve months. We would now be paying one hundred and five dollars more. We just got robbed. We seriously considered going to their local office and shooting a few people. We decided to delay that action until we could find out who was the top leader of this band of thieves. We disconnected the computer and gave it to our neighbor's teenage son. We disconnected the T.V. and gave it to the old lady that lives down the road. We were taking back our lives. We were not going to be forced to pay for mindless media garbage. Friday was horrible. I got a speeding ticket on my way to the farmer's market. I was blazing eight miles over the speed limit. The cop had a real bad attitude. At the market, a tired looking mother was so mean to her children. A man beat his young dog for cocking his leg and pissing on a tire. You could see he had no love for that dog; the dog was a gadget to prance around the market with. Then a hyena man bumped me with his shoulder so that he could get to the peaches that he had his eyes on. When I got home and was unloading the car, a polite black teenager came and tried to hustle me to buy a magazine subscription so that he could use the profits to go to college. When I told him we already had more magazines than we really needed; he started the usual black routine. The once polite teenager turned into a scowling mask of anger and practiced indignation. You must not like black people; you probably are prejudiced like most white people. You know the regular routine. Our lunch at the local too-expensive steak house had to have been stolen from the nearby homeless shelter. We decided to have dinner at a nice restaurant, Al's, to celebrate the end of a terrible week. This great restaurant has a booth right next to the restrooms and across from the kitchen and of course our name was written in black smoke right over that booth. It would really be a stretch to call the girl that waited on us a waitress. The food was O.K. even with the mixture of the nearby restroom odors. When we left this imposter of a fine restaurant; we were robbed at gunpoint as we were getting in the car. The robber was the black teenage magazine hustler. The police that responded to the scene of the crime looked like two galoots that were flying high. We prayed when we got home safely."

Shady's high shrieking laugh could be heard back in the cafeteria kitchen. "I can't wait to hear about the weekend."

Deputy Aaron said, "Let's start wrapping it up gentlemen."

The stranger pushed his chair back to get ready to leave, said, "I thought I had controlled my emotions and had pushed all of the negativity out of my mind. Saturday morning I raced in the annual 5K race to raise funds for the local schools. I had been training for weeks. I won the race in my age group and I was second overall. When I went to get my cheap plastic trophy, the trophy purveyor told me that I was disqualified because I had run the race listening to my music on my headphones. This race now had a no headphone policy. Everything got slow and turned to black and white and before I could control my emotions, my eager fist broke his jaw. I was arrested and got three months for assault and battery. I was lucky; they wanted to prosecute me for a hate crime. How was I to know he was a swish?"

The stranger stood up and extended his hand to Shady and said, "This is my last day. I get out tomorrow."

Shady grabbed and shook the stranger's hand said, "Man, it's been great talking to you. Should I just call you The Panty Man?"

"Sure that's as good as any name."

As the stranger turned to leave, Shady said, "The Panty Man. Good Luck to the great Mr. Panty Man."

The stranger exited the cafeteria's side door reserved for special prisoners. Deputy Aaron turned and yelled, "Hey, Junius, you can close up shop." Junius rushed over to the blinding white table, he threw his elbows on the table top, hunched over and leaned forward and said, "Stick, you crazy son a bitch. Man why you talking to that killing fiend. I can't believe Deputy Aaron let you sit with him. Deputy Aaron must hate you. What the hell you were thinking."

Perplexed at the concern in Junius's voice, Stick said, "What the hell, that's the Panty Man, that's not a killer."

Biting his bottom lip and balling his fist, Junius pounded the table top and yelled, "The Panty Man hell! Man, you stupid. How in the hell have you've lived this long. That's Wayne the Waster. He's in the joint for killing people. "

Stick's face turned into a puzzled veil of disappointment, "He's a killer?"

Junius buffed the table top to either clean it or to rub out his glaring reflection, rocked his head back and forth and said, "That's right. Drug deal gone badly; everyone dead. A father bought the killer's motorcycle for his two sons with a bad check. The whole family is still missing. He warned his neighbor, that he barely escaped an attack by his pit bull that had been terrorizing the neighborhood. The neighbor turned the water hose on him and laughed as he drenched your friend. The next night the neighbor's house burnt down with him still in his bed. You want more stories? You better watch yourself, boy."

Shaking his head in disbelief, Stick was angry with himself. Once again he foolishly thought everyone was his friend and once again he was duped.

Shaking his finger at Stick, Junius said, "And that ain't anything. Stick I'm telling you to stay away from that assassin. Two brothers got in an argument with him over some damn magazines. They told him when the guards were not around, that they were going to mess him up. The next morning those two brothers were found in their locked cell with their heads cut off. Their cell was locked. Junius slapped his damp towel on the table top said, "Let me tell you one more thing about your new good friend. Bout a month ago, this giant tattooed muscle freak was saying loudly that anyone that practiced yoga was a fruity bitch. The massive animal was looking for a fight and he knew your friend practiced his yoga every day. The tattooed muscle freak took a sip of his tea and started choking. Your friend's eyes were locked on the muscle freak's eyes. He choked to death in front of everyone right here in this cafeteria in front of everyone. You could see that the killer took over the muscle freak's thoughts. It was crazy, I felt like I was in a Star Wars movie. That's why they don't let him eat here when there are other people. I always look down at my feet when the devil walks by me."

Red faced and embarrassed, Stick said, "He said he was getting out tomorrow."

Junius quickly turned to face Shady and his lips once again slammed open to reveal an all teeth and gums smile rattled out, "He ain't ever getting out of here. When he dies they gonna bury his butt here on the Farm."

Stick slowly rose from the white table shaking his head in disbelief. He couldn't help feeling foolish and hoodwinked again. He was serving time for being so gullible and trusting. He liked falling into easy conversation with friends and strangers but he must learn to be wary of everyone. He felt disappointed when he realized that he should be cautious of everyone. He sadly smiled to himself when he thought: All for none and none for all. Everyone is out to take your money or your scalp. As Stick walked out of the cafeteria doors he turned and said, "Don't worry Junius, I won't be eating with the Panty Man again."

Two weeks later.

Walking at a quick pace, Stick was in a hurry so that he could get to work on time. He was feeling good about himself because of his recent promotion. Some of his colleagues had worked at the Farm's warehouse for thirty years and he was promoted over all of them. Many of the inmates working in the warehouse were docile criminals that needed some type of assistant living. They had to scratch and claw on the outside, but thrived in an environment of enforced rules. It was amazing to Stick that such a large number of inmates couldn't read or write, but were successful when coached on how and when to do something. After he signed in and grabbed a cup of coffee he bounded up the stairs to his spartan office. A chair and a small desk and his own T.V. were the only furnishings in his new office. Every morning he sat in his surprisingly cozy and comfortable chair, drank his first cup of coffee and turned on the TV to listen to the morning news.. As he settled into his chair, his favorite beautiful newswoman appeared on the TV. She was standing outside a bank. He took a sip of his coffee and choked to get it down.

The newswoman said, "Hello this is Karen Penn with station WBUU reporting from the First National Bank. Yes, it has been confirmed that the Panty Man is alive and well. This morning he robbed the First National Bank of an undisclosed amount of cash. Police said they are sure it's the notorious bank robber because of surveillance footage and the teller's description of a tattoo. The police are not saying what the tattoo looks like or where it's located. They did say the teller said that the robber said that he had chosen their bank because it was so shady inside. They are not sure what that meant. The police are asking that if you recognize the man in the photo; please contact them at the number at the bottom of this picture. This is Karen Penn with station WBUU, and back to you Rick."

Frozen in his chair, mouth hanging open and goose bumps rapidly and pleasantly spreading across his body, Stick whispered to himself, "Hot damn, I can't believe it. It's the Panty Man and in striped drawers. He was telling me hello when he said it was shady inside." He then sat there just staring at the TV.

Suddenly the door to Stick's office opened, Officer David stuck his head in and said, "Come on Stick, you know the rules, no TV during work hours. Turn off that TV and let's get to work."

Stick lowered his head and said, "Yes sir, Officer David."

When Officer David closed the door, Stick stood up and a thought kept racing through his mind, "No more frivolous rules; I want to be free like the Panty Man."

May 2011

PLEASE BELIEVE ME

(It May Be My Only Chance)

My name is Augustine Badeaux and, unfortunately, you will probably not believe the story that I am about to tell you. Why am
I so sure that you will see this story as fiction? If I were you and you
were me and you told me this crazy story, I would just laugh and rec-
ommend that you get some help. In the future I would try to avoid you.
But you will have to decide: a madman, a charlatan or someone begging
you to believe. The following story is true and told with the best of my
memory.

Augustine's week had been good but busy, and he was very tired
on this Friday night. He planned on sleeping-in on Saturday morning
to recharge his tired body and mind. He had set the air conditioning to
sixty-eight degrees. He slept best in a cool room under a heavy blanket.
When his wife, Cathy, had bought the satin sheets he was not sure if
he'd like the way they would feel. But now he loved the way they felt
once his body warmed the sheets. Augustine encased himself into his
pale green, cool, smooth, glossy shroud, pulled the blanket to his neck,
snuggled up to Cathy and was soon asleep. When the morning's soft
light greeted him, he noticed that Cathy had already gotten up; so he
turned over, stretched and thought, "Ooh this feels so good, so silky lus-
cious, like a velvet cocoon. I feel so warm; everything is so warm and
soft. I could do this forever. I could just stretch like a cat, turn over and
sleep for a sensuous eternity. I am so ......" Suddenly his life changed
forever.

From total contentment to dizzy confusion, Augustine grabbed the
bed to steady himself; but the bed was not there. He opened his eyes

and was stunned to see thousands of people walking past him. Fear and confusion were racing through his mind, he whispered to himself, "My God what has just happened to me." Terror was beginning to build in his chest. He feebly said in a fear-infected voice, "Help!" The people, most dressed in their finest, flowed past Augustine and gazed at him with an understanding smile. Fear was crushing the bottom of his spine; he was unable to move, only capable of watching the river of people walk past him. Like a beggar on the side of the street, with an outstretched hand, Augustine could barely blurt out, "Help. Help me, please." When no one came to his rescue his breathing became quicker. He felt like he was suffocating, couldn't swallow and was about to get sick all over his favorite midnight blue expensive suit. Augustine was jolted back to reality for a brief moment, "My suit. Why am I in my favorite suit?" He always thought of himself as a man's man, a rugged individual, but now his body was shaking and he felt like crying. He could usually steel himself and fight off unnecessary emotions. But this was so sudden, so unexpected that he needed help. He needed a friend. Just before the blackness could close up his consciousness, an image, a mirage appeared before him. Because of the rapidly changing horror of events, he was having a hard time focusing on the person standing before him. Fighting to stay conscious, he weakly stretched out his hand toward the image and said, "Help me! Please!"

The image came closer and spoke to the saucer-eyed frightened man. "Hello, my name is Mignon." In a doctorally demeanor she said, "Sit up straight, I want you to focus on the tip of my finger. Now breathe deep through your nose." Augustine robotically complied. "Hold that breath. O.K. now very slowly breathe out through your mouth. Let's do it again." When Mignon saw that Augustine was calming down she said, "Slowly take your focus off of my finger and look at me." Augustine slowly turned his head to look at his savior. He saw an angelic face with wild golden red hair, Icelandic white skin and ivy green eyes. Her white sleeveless slip gently moved in the breeze. She seemed to be hovering over him like an angel.

Augustine's eyes suddenly ripped wide open and said, "Are you an angel?"

Mignon's small but sensuous lips parted and she softly said, "My name is Mignon and I am your temporary guide."

Regaining some cognitive functions, Augustine said with an air of disbelief, "What? Is this some kind of sex dream?"

Her delicate laugh tinkled the air, "Augustine what do you think is happening? Do you really believe that you are dreaming?"

"What's wrong with me? What is happening to me?"

Mignon drew closer to Augustine and held his hand in a grip of compassion, "This is never easy to explain. But when I am through it may be easier for you to understand than it will be to accept your situation.

A cold shiver of fear coursed through his body, "My situation?"

Her fingers of her right hand lifted Augustine's chin until his eyes were level with her arresting green eyes. Augustine, ever the attention deficit, noticed the childlike smallness of Mignon's fingers. Re-leveling his gaze into her eyes, Mignon softly said, "Augustine, what is the last thing you can remember before awakening in this meadow?"

Not hearing the whole question, Augustine said, "How do you know my name?"

Smiling and happy that Augustine was a questioner and not an orders-taking servant said, "Augustine, I will answer all of your questions but first you must answer my questions so that I can help you understand. Now, what is the last thing that you remember?"

Augustine tilted his head downward and closed his eyes and thought, "I was sleeping. I was just sleeping-in for the morning. Yes I was sleeping, so this must be a dream."

She gave him an encouraging smile, "Good, now what date is it?" She could see that his mind was wandering and firmly ordered, "No questions Augustine; what is the date today?"

His mind was paralyzed; he closed his eyes to concentrate. He stammered, "It must be May 9th since I was at my brother's birthday party yesterday."

Pleased with his cooperation, Mignon quickly said, "What year?"

Knitting his brow in agitation and beginning to lose patience he said, "2011."

Trying to keep him on track and not giving him a chance to mentally wander, she barked, "What did you do once you left the party?"

Wanting to please this beautiful woman, his beautiful fairy god-mother, he eagerly responded, "We drove home; I had a shower, ate some cereal and then went to bed."

Mignon quickly surmised that Augustine had died in his sleep. Some people had all the luck, to go so peacefully, to be so blind to, or maybe deprived of the mental horrors moments before death. To live death, prepares you for the eventual finality. "How long; how long did you sleep?"

Augustine moved from sitting to kneeling on one knee and wanted some answers, "Eight hours, maybe nine. What's going on? What's happening? I just want to go home." His voice broke into a scared scream, "Tell me what is happening, please, please."

Taking a moment to do the math in her head, Mignon said, "Augustine, to the best of my calculation you have been sleeping for over four thousand five hundred years, maybe longer."

Wondering if this was what mental illness felt like, Augustine yelled, "Rip Van Winkle?"

A little giggle spread her beautiful lips into a smile, "You would not believe how often that statement is used. Anyone that lived in the last third of the second millennium or the first half of the third knows the last part of that story."

Unable to contain his fearful impatience, Augustine took a deep calming breath and growled, "Listen to me. No more questions. Just explain to me what is happening and who are you and what the hell am I doing here? What the hell is going on? Please give me some damn answers."

Realizing that she hadn't done that good of a job preparing Augustine, Mignon knew that it was unfair to not take each and every encounter seriously. It may actually hurt her final judgment. Judgment, if that is what actually happens?

Sitting in the lush meadow grass, Mignon folded her arms close to her breast and with a slight tremor in her voice said, "Augustine, I will tell you everything I know and then you can make your own decision.

Probably the best place to start is to tell you a little about me. My name is Mignon Fratelli. I was from the ancient city of Quebec. I say ancient city because by the time I roamed her streets, Quebec was over one thousand years old. During your time Quebec was a city in the country of Canada. Probably around 2080 or 2090 or maybe 2100, I not too sure of the dates since it happened so long ago; but at about this time is when the western part of Canada succeeded from the eastern part of the country. It had something to do about oil. Eventually the western parts of Canada joined the old United States of America. Quebec was part of New Gaul. I was born in the year 2953. It was a great time to be alive. The world was at peace. The planet's population had its excesses under control. Abject poverty had been eliminated. In the early part of the millennium the two lower classes were treated as peasants. The Golden Calf was still the religion for many men. During my era there was still a three social class system, but everyone was a partner in the drive for the nearly impossible ideal society. It was a beautiful time. The planet had begun to heal and for the first time in mankind's' history she truly became our mother, tired but beautiful. My life was almost perfect. I was in love. I was really in love for the first time. I had a wonderful and important job. I was a French teacher for third-tier students. But life always has her scales to give some good with some bad. Unfortunately for me when she decided to balance her scales she went a little too heavy on one side. The bad happened so suddenly. Society had done a good job with the emotion of greed. But I think the human species will always be cursed by the emotion of jealously. The day that it happened feels like it was yesterday."

Kneeling in front of Mignon, Augustine was devouring each word that came from her mouth and said, "The day, what happened?"

Showing her teacher's experience and patience, she lifted her hand to silence him, "Augustine I will tell you everything that I can remember. It was an ordinary day. I woke early, walked to my parents' house to have breakfast with them. I left right after breakfast so that I could get to the market before the predicted rainstorm made its mess. By the time I got home the wind was shooting stinging raindrops at me. I unloaded my groceries and then decided to change into something more comfortable. As soon as I walked into my bedroom I saw him. I could smell my fear. I was too paralyzed to run. In a near scream I shouted, "Tomas what are you doing here." Tomas leaped out of the chair and slapped me hard across the face and said, "Shut up bitch." I had thought I was through with this possessive man. Grabbing me by the hair he pulled me within inches of his snarling face. When I saw his eyes I knew I was going to die. Augustine I don't want to relive this horror. He was a companion I had liked, until I saw his violent personality. He didn't mind that I refused to see him, but he grew into a jealous rage when I began seeing another man. He had brought a knife and the first time he stabbed me, he timidly thrust it about two inches into my stomach. When he saw the fear on my face, he became bolder and stabbed me again, but this time much deeper. As painful as my wounds were, the overwhelming feeling was uncontrolled fear with a black doom spreading through my consciousness. I no longer looked at Tomas as he stabbed me again and again. Fear had crippled my mind as I meekly laid there. Augustine I remember my death and you do not seem to remember when you died. That's why I believe you died in your sleep."

Augustine had never in his life listened to a story so intently. His mouth was open as he uttered, "What happened next?"

Looking at the river of people passing by, Mignon thought to herself, "Why? Why do I have to constantly relive this horror? What is the purpose? Am I supposed to learn something? I need a little more help. Please help me one more time."

Seeing the pain on Mignon's face, Augustine said, "I know this is difficult for you, but give me just a little more help."

Her green eyes floating in tears, Mignon spoke gently, "I will give you all the help that I can."

He was no longer just thinking of himself. He wanted to hold her, to comfort her, but he still needed answers so with a solemn face Augustine said, "Did you go into a dreamy sleep?"

Mignon took a deep breath and looked away, "I knew I had died and that I was in this peaceful regret-free rest. I didn't think about what had happened or what might be next. It felt like I rested for about a day. Then I awoke in this meadow. I was terrified just as you were.

My guide's name was Esma. The human species was still surviving in the year 5027. That was the year that he died. He also could remember his death. They had just rediscovered electricity and didn't have any safety standards. He was electrocuted. He told me that almost all religions speak of an afterlife. Augustine, welcome to the resurrection, the end." Then as a question with outstretched hands she said, "The final judgment?"

Augustine silently mouthed the word, "What?"

Looking at her open hands that were now lying in her lap she said, "Everyone you see walking in this peaceful meadow on this ever perfect day has died and have awoken. They have risen from the dead. Are their bodies and of course our bodies still lying in some cold concrete tomb or rotting in the mother earth. I don't know. I have met people who died in the first through the sixth millennium. Most are dressed in their funeral glory. If you look closely you will see that many have no clothes. What was their death like? Where is this moving mass going? What is their final destination? What will happen to them when they get to this final destination? Who or what will be at the end? I can give you no answers to those questions. My guide Esma could only guess as I am doing now. All I can suggest is to assume that your religion was partly correct. I guess we will eventually find out if the worlds' religions were totally accurate.

Feeling part anger and part fear coming out of him Augustine yelled, "Why are you doing this to me? This doesn't make sense and I really don't want to be talking to you about the food for fools, at a time like this."

She had been through this same argument thousands of times and she could only frown and say, "My friend we all have to deal with this in his or her own way. I know this is extremely confusing. Believe me the panic will subside. He spoke to me and I still have questions."

Showing anger, Augustine snarled, "Oh no, please don't tell me you some kind of Jesus freak. He spoke to you. What a lucky freak. Give me some of your drugs so he can speak to me."

Mignon knew this anger; she had seen this frustration many times. She never had good answers. Why was she chosen when she lacked the skills to convince? "I can only tell you what happened. After my guide, Esma, told me everything that he knew I stepped into the river of man to seek my destination. I didn't know what to expect, but I was determined to seek out my destiny. As I flowed with this tide I could see the panorama of human history all around me. I felt like everyone was a brother, a sister, they were my family. Did I walk for a day or one hundred years? It was not my body, but my mind that marched on. It was all so beautiful, so peaceful. I know that doesn't make sense to you, but it will. Suddenly my mind, my consciousness, seemed bright and awake. It felt like I was learning something for the first time. Then it happened. I could visualize the words that were shaking me awake. The words were, *you did not do enough, you must help, you must explain, you must send them to me.* I froze, then the words were spoken to me, "You did not do enough, you must help, you must explain, you must send them to me. I kept waiting for more, but I never got another vision or heard any mind-voice again. When I helped my first confused passenger, it felt good. I call these people passengers walking through this meadow. Passengers in a vehicle called life and death. The vehicle that gives you the ultimate ride."

Never able to stomach a debate on religion, Augustine stood up to confront this angelic beauty, "So this all powerful whatever didn't come to you and directly speak to you. He didn't even have the decency to throw in a burning bush. I think we are both hallucinating."

Standing directly in front of Augustine, Mignon said, "Augustine, I never said anything about an all-powerful whatever. Your doubt, your refusal to believe is only natural. I am always amazed at the people that listen to my explanation and their only question is to ask what to do next. I can. I can understand you being a Doubter."

Finding strength through his anger he protested, "Doubter? This is what I don't understand about all religions. Why does this all powerful god or whatever you want to call him have to speak in riddles? Why can't he just come before the people and give specific directions. Why speak through a carpenter or a merchant? He spoke to Abraham, Mohammad, Moses, Jesus, Noah and countless others. Why the hell can't he speak to me? I have always wanted to believe. I don't want my world to end.

I don't want everything to be over, but I could never believe based on faith alone. Some people say that if you don't have faith, then you have nothing, because there is nothing else. That statement brings fear to my heart. I want to cry when I hear that statement because I realize they know no more than I."

Mignon turned to step closer to the passing river of mankind and with her back to him she said, "Maybe he or her or as you say, the whatever, has come before with directions. Over the generations we begin to forget and we begin to believe that these stories and these rules are myths. I wish I had more answers for you."

Given the opportunity to vent his fear and anger Augustine followed Mignon closer to the edge of the human river and said, "I can tell you what I do believe. I believe we were born to die, a guaranteed experience. Some people live a short sweet existence; but for many people life is just a mundane unlucky eternity with a final outcome of grateful, but scared, relief."

Mignon turned to face him and she wore a mischievous smile, a type of smile Augustine always called a Delvin the Devil smile. It was a smile that put you on alert. "Do you believe in the Bible?"

Looking down at the seraphim he spoke slowly but forcefully, "I truly dislike people that use the Bible or any holy book as their invincible weapon. They slash at all debate with their best seller. I believe people's invention of religion, heaven and hell is their desire for immortality or their dread of a finite end. It's their desire, not reality." Augustine raised his hands in a pleading gesture and said, "Why? Why is life so short for some? Why is it so horrible for others? Why does this black horrifying doom settle over much of the world? Why do good people as you suffer so?"

Grasping his pleading hands, Mignon looked into his eyes and spoke gracefully, "Augustine I wish I could answer all of your questions. I am as confused as everyone else. Even those who have all the answers have a fleeting glimpse of doubt and many have just given up and have taken the easier route and become fervent followers. For me accepting God was not the same as accepting religion. Accepting God was accepting an attitude of satisfaction with my life-no fear and no dread, accepting myself and being thankful for life and the experience of each day. Maybe that's too passive for you, but that is a close description of my philosophy."

Holding Mignon's small hands calmed Augustine. He shook his head, "I just need things that I can see and touch. It could be so much easier.

Mignon encircled her arm around his lower back, leaned her face on his upper arm and led Augustine into the human river. In her soothing velvety voice she said, "The only without–a-doubt answer I can give you is that at the end of this journey will be the answers you are looking for. We had to live, and then we had to die and now we will find what is next on this journey. You must flow in this river to meet your destiny. Be thankful that there is more and that you are now on a journey of discovery."

Sensing that his only friend would be leaving he said in a shaky voice, "What do you believe is next?

Her head still resting against his arm said, "My father who was a medical researcher said that if you minimally understood the endless complexes of the brain and the brilliant simplistic use of DNA, then you would realize that nature is God. There was a plan, a blueprint, from the mind of an unimaginable genius."

Thoughts racing through his mind, Augustine couldn't help but think how he had wasted so much of his life on silly stuff, on frivolous worries. If he could only have another chance, but this time with specific rules and guidelines, he would make every day count. Ignoring one of his biggest rants about how most people receive too many second chances, he could only plead for one more chance at life. He again looked at Mignon and tried to show courage and forced a worry-stressed smile. He sighed, "What should I do next?"

Her stoic smile cracked just a bit and was grateful that Augustine was intelligent enough to know that she would not hold his hand forever. Bracing herself for the end of another wonderful encounter, she said, "Augustine, I have been a guide for many thousands of times. Is this my heaven or my hell?" Mignon removed a gold band with dark green stones from her finger and was barely able to stuff Augustine's right little finger into her prized possession, then tears racing down her cheeks, Mignon kept her eyes on the ring and cried, "When you meet him or her or as you say, the whatever, please give my ring to our Father or our Mother. Maybe he will call me home." She stretched to kiss him on the check and then turned and was swallowed by the swarming river of history.

Once again his nightmare had become ominous. Standing in his haunted loneliness, his frightened mind was shutting down all senses. Augustine turned to face his future; he heard nothing and the silence only got louder. The colors of the river, black, green, blue, white and pink folded brightly as they engulfed him. Stiff-legged and at a snail's pace, he began to walk to his destiny. His philosophy had always been if there is no way out, then go forward. Once he convinced himself that no super being could fault him for the small indiscretions that he had committed, his walk became a little more confident. He had been thinking inside the box, maybe he had to focus his thoughts outside of the box. The more he focused, the more it became a mental challenge, the quicker his step became. Maybe all was not what it seemed. He always liked to brain storm his ideas with other people; especially people that liked to chip away at his theories. For the first time, Augustine looked closely at the marching human army. He was surprised at the many shades of white, the different hues of black, from lightly tanned to a copper brown; such a variety of skin tones using such limited pigments. All Mankind was so similar with limitless variety. He studied the faces and saw fear on many and acceptance on others. With crushing loneliness, he thought how comforting it would be to experience this adventure with someone he knew. Then at that moment and with that thought he was thunderstruck by what he saw. "Oh no, not him; Wayne is that you?"

The usual ear to ear closed-lipped smile was there, and his eyes popped wide with recognition and excitement, then Wayne shouted, "Augustine! Augustine Badeaux! Hey man is this something? I'm stunned. This is more, much more than I ever expected. I'm so glad to see someone I know. I can't believe this wonder. I have met people from everywhere, from all eras of history. You know me, the all-time greatest wallflower. But this has awakened something in my dead soul. I feel like I'm riding on a beam of light."

Augustine did not understand the enthusiasm, thinking this perennial nut was probably tripping on some pyscho drug questioned, "Wayne of all people, I would have thought you would be a little more concerned about the gravity of our situation."

The silly shut-tight smile was still there and his eyes had a glimmer. Wayne laughed, "Oh Augustine, there was a lot of debauchery, a little laziness and a few conflicts with the Commandments, but I was never a Judas or a Jabez Stone. No Augustine, I am not afraid of doomsday. I've even had my own personal guiding angel. She was beautiful, a little redhead with grab-you green eyes; a Gallic beauty. Some people call this mass migration a river. Not me, I call it my road. My road to find out, to drink that promised fourth cup of wine with Jesus and Augustine, you're welcome to join this traveling circus."

He followed Wayne on his newfound quest of brotherhood to all mankind. He walked with Wayne and his brotherhood of fellow travelers for hundreds of years or maybe it was just a few minutes. It was a very interesting road show that eliminated his fear of the mystery. Eventually he became so overwhelmed with the need to solve this mystery that he started running. He now realized why at random someone would just burst out from the pack and start running. He now understood that they were ready for it to end. He was ready for the mystery to end. He was ready to atone for his misdeeds; to pay reparations if he must. He didn't know how long he ran, but it felt like a five minute year. Then suddenly it happened. He felt the frisson vibrate down his spine; his mind was awake like never before. Then he saw it as he heard it: *you make the rules, you live by the guidelines.* His body froze into an awaiting statute. Listing and looking for more. Then in his state of bewilderment he started to cry. Standing in the middle of the human traffic, he looked up at the perfect swirls of blue and said, "Why?" In his mind he kept repeating the word why. He had been ready for the end. He was ready to meet his maker. He wanted the mystery to be over. He thought that this river of people was the infinite cycle of creation. But what did this mean? What did, you make the rules, mean? Why couldn't someone sit with him and explain? Why something couldn't be written down or etched into stone. Yes it was burned into his thoughts, but what does it mean?

The sunshine that streamed into the bedroom had a late morning glow. A thin woman wrapped in a man's bathrobe was kneeling next to the bed.

"Wake up Honey. Is everything O.K.?" Augustine's wife Cathy spoke softly only inches from his face and petted his hair, she kept repeating, "Augustine get up, you're starting to scare me. Come on, sit up." Augustine half opened his eyes; he had the facial expression of a drowning survivor silently gasping for air.

He slowly opened his searching eyes and said, "I'm O.K."

Still kneeling by the side of the bed, a concerned expression on her face, Cathy pulled the blanket out of Augustine's clenched fist. "Baby you were scaring me. You were sleeping so hard, you seemed like you were dead."

Concentrating on his breath he closed his eyes and said, "I'm O.K. Sweetie, I'm O.K."

Staring at his face, still stroking his hair she searched for an answer, "You didn't drink much alcohol last night. Is it a hangover? You seemed fine when we went to bed. You scared me. You were so unconscious. Augie are you O.K.?"

Slowly moving his head back and forth, but still too weak to have a conversation he weakly said, "Yes."

Still on her knees, her hands rested on his thighs and intently she searched his face for clues. "Baby, why are you wearing your favorite suit? When did you get dressed? Your feet are poking out of the covers, so except for being shoeless you are dressed for some important meeting. Are you worried about your job? I'm worried about you. Talk to me."

He wasn't feeling strong enough to have a coherent conversation so to be alone, in a weak congested voice he said, "Can I have a cup of coffee?"

Relieved to be given a task, Cathy stood and said, "I've had it ready for two hours. Don't move. I'll be right back."

Augustine slowly sat on the side of the bed, elbows on his thighs he cradled his face in his hands and thought, "Was this a too-real nightmare, what else could it be?"

Cathy hurriedly walked into the bedroom that she had made for herself and the only one she ever loved. As she walked into her lair, steam from the cup of coffee lazily trailed behind her. She knelt in front of Augustine to hand him the cup of coffee and said, "Here Baby, here's your coffee. Augie what's that ring on your little finger?"

He looked down at his little finger and saw a gold band with small forest green stones embedded in the center of the band encircling his finger. He could barely hear Cathy saying, "It's too small. It's cutting off the circulation. You better take it off before your finger begins to swell."

He had been holding his breath and now a loud rush of air escaped. He could feel a heavy sadness gripping his heart as he lay back across the bed and started crying.

Cathy quickly stood up and pleaded, "Baby let me help you. You're scaring me. Please let me help you."

"That was three months ago. It's been ridiculous around here. First I had to reestablish Cathy's confidence that I was there for us. I had to assure her that I experienced a too-real nightmare, but I was O.K. Then I had to sort out what had happened to me. I still have a lingering hope that it was just a horrifically real nightmare. I've convinced Cathy but I can't convince myself. Now I'm having trouble suppressing my anger. I just wanted some simple answers. You make the rules; you live by the guidelines, what the hell does that mean? He told Noah to build a boat; he told Abraham to kill his kid and I get a damn riddle. Why not send me on a mission, a hero mission? Was I given a mission? What does it mean? Cathy caught me loudly cursing and then pleading to an audience-free room. I'm so lucky to be married to someone like Cathy. I am overjoyed to be back with her. It's a relief to have a best friend by your side, but she is more than a best friend, she is part of my soul. She would fight the Devil to protect me. I can see she still has some reservations about my mental well-being. Last night she said that she thinks someone must have put something in my drink at the party." Twice last night she said, "Go slow, breathe deep and focus, soon everything will be O.K." "I know she is upset that I took a leave of absence from my job. But I have to concentrate on what is my mission. You make the rules. Does that mean I have to compete with Moses and his Commandments? There is already a Golden Rule. Do I create a deluxe Golden Rule? I know that she's beginning to get scared again, but I will be O.K. once I solve this stupid riddle. I just wanted simple answers and the mystery still survives. It's obvious that I am just grasping in the dark. I am so grateful to have been made aware that there is more to life; but also angry over my total confusion. Are you laughing yet? Are you calling me a dunderhead, Augustine the confused prophet? Maybe you are saying that Augustine is a bad writer of nonsense. Are you thinking I should be crucified for wasting your time? If I were you I would be angry for reading another story about the hereafter and still not getting any concrete touchable answers. Am I asking you to have faith? No, absolutely not. Faith is a puzzle, an enigma; no I could never ask anyone to have confidence in a journey that still has me confused. But this really happened, please believe me, I may not be a good storyteller, but listen, search and you will find others that have had nearly the same experience. I didn't write this story to entertain you; I wrote it to inform you. After reading this story, I hope it provides clues to help you solve the mystery. I have never been good at unraveling riddles, so I would gladly accept help. I started this story begging you to believe me. I am ending this story asking you to believe me. Believe me for a better world and for me to find my personal answer to the mystery. I believe it's my only chance. "

"By the way Wayne is back. I have not spoken to him. I saw him from a distance and he was still smiling and it looked like he was wearing a collar."

January 2011

THE RETURN

June 12, 2012—6:05 A.M.—Thibodaux, Louisiana—Ozema's Morning Café

*T*he pale, barely visible sunbeams penetrate the café's dining room
lightly illuminating early morning diners preparing for their work
day. Workmen and women dressed in their work uniforms, some in suits,
some in overalls huddle around their tables engaged in hushed conversa-
tion, others are readers enjoying the morning newspaper and then there
are the ones that just stare at one of the three televisions always turned
to a news station with the volume turned to a barely audible level. Diners
at Ozema's are a quiet group and Ozema Bergeron wouldn't have it any
other way. The sounds of hushed conversation in early morning voices
can be heard at different levels but never over an early morning polite-
ness. The dominant sounds of the café are dishes clacking into each other,
forks tinging plates, coffee cups being seated in saucers keeping a con-
stant beat and the occasional sizzle from the kitchen provided the early
morning orchestral score. The smells of toast, beignets, pancakes and cane
syrup swirled through the cafe but the constant comforting background
smell has always been fresh brewed coffee. This Tuesday morning was like
any other early morning at 6:05 A.M. until all eyes focused on the barely
audible newscaster's lips:

"We are interrupting your early morning programming to bring
you this breaking and still developing news. We have confirmed
reports that NORAD, the North American Aerospace Defense
Command, a joint Canadian and U.S Defense Command that provides aerospace warning and defense for the two countries detected
at 4:04 A.M. Eastern Standard Time a possible unfriendly launch

of a missile originating from the area of southwestern Venezuela or eastern Columbia. This missile, if it was a missile, disappeared 3 minutes after launch. NORAD is on high alert and has fighter jets from the U.S. Northern Command patrolling the southern portions of continental United States airspace. We have been told that NORAD with its worldwide system of sensors designed to give the leaders of Canada and the United States an accurate picture of aerospace or maritime threats is in constant contact with the President. Good Morning, a frightening start to the day; my name is Charlie Ritz sitting in for Walter Highkite. We are still waiting for word from the White House. Our White House correspondent, Bill Elderson, is standing by waiting for a statement."

Charlie: "Bill, any word yet when we might hear a White House explanation of these events."

Bill: "Good Morning Charlie. A junior aide to White House Press Secretary, Henry Reagen, just ambled over to the podium and said that because of the continual flow of new information a statement has been delayed for at least fifteen minutes."

Charlie: "Bill, we have unconfirmed reports that the President boarded Air Force One and has left the D.C. area "

Bill: "We have no confirmation on that or for anything else. It's kind of eerie around here. Most of Washington is usually coming to life at this time of the morning; but it feels deserted or abandoned. All I can really tell you is a repeat of what you just said. At 4:04 A.M. Eastern Standard Time NORAD detected a launch of an object, missile or rocket, we're not exactly sure, with an unknown destination and after tracking it for about three minutes it just disappeared. We don't know if it reached its destination, blew up, or had some failure and just dropped into the ocean."

Charlie: "Bill, stand by. We have some information from Diane Hamner, our correspondent in Paris. Diane can you hear me; are you there?"

Diane Hamner: "Yea Charlie, I can hear you. Charlie, I'm standing outside the European Space Agency's headquarters here in Paris. The Space Agency put out a statement about ten minutes ago. The statement basically says that about two hours ago the Agency's Space Center called the Ariane Launch Control Center located in Kourou, French Guiana detected a missile launch that was aimed in the direction of the United States."

Charlie: "Diane, for the sake of our viewers, where is French Guiana?"

Diane: "Charlie, it's in South America, on Brazil's northern border on the Atlantic coast. It was once a French colony and may still be, I'm not sure of that status. But Charlie, this news is now on all French news channels and we're getting reports that this story is being broadcast in Great Britain and Spain. The mystery Charlie is what has happened to that missile?"

Charlie: "Have they said where the launch originated?"

Diane: "The statement just says that the launch was detected west of the country of French Guiana and Charlie we're now getting word from other reporters around us that the agency is not sure if it was a missile."

Charlie: "Diane! Diane! Thank you and get back to us with any new information. We're going back to the White House. Bill, what you got for us?"

Bill: "Charlie we're getting word that NASA, the European Space Agency and the Kremlin all received reports from the International Space Station that at about 4:06 E.S.T. alarms went off in the Station and in Houston because the Station was on a possible collision course with, at the time, was an unknown object. The astronauts could see this object enter their trajectory, stay stationary for a few moments, then a small flash, and it just disappeared."

Charlie: "Bill, are they saying if this flash was an explosion?"

Bill: "No Charlie, NASA has said that they don't believe an explosion occurred. There was absolutely no debris, nothing and Charlie the astronauts said it didn't look like a missile. They described it as a swirling gray disturbance. The Space Station is orbiting earth at over two hundred miles up. If it was a missile it would have to be an intercontinental ballistic missile. Charlie, am I correct? Wouldn't it have to be a very sophisticated missile to get – wait Charlie, Press Secretary Henry Reagen is stepping up to the podium."

Henry Reagen: "Good Morning folks, it's been some morning hasn't it? I'm going to read to you a statement that has been prepared and then answer any questions that I can. At 4:04 A.M. EST, NORAD, the North American Defense Command, detected a launch of, what we believe, to be a missile and possibly a ballistic missile. The missile was on a path that could have possibly taken it to New York City or the D.C. area. The likely launch site was the border of Columbia and Venezuela. Both countries are denying that a missile was launched by their governments. In fact, both governments have said that they don't even have missiles in their arsenals. The missile launch was spotted by both conventional land and sea radar. We can confirm reports that astronauts on the International Space Station did see the missile. Three minutes after launch the missile possibly had a malfunction and disappeared from radar. We do have military personnel stationed in Columbia and they are in route to the launch area. At this time we are still gathering intelligence and as things become clearer to us we'll let you know. I will take a couple of questions and then I will be back with more news in about thirty minutes.

Bill Elderson: "Mr. Reagen, you said that the astronauts saw a missile. The Kremlin and the European Space agency are saying that they saw something but it was not a missile."

Henry Reagen: "Well let me clarify that they said they saw something. They are not sure what they saw."

Bill Elderson: "We are getting reports that they saw an explosion."

BBC Reporter George Windsor: "Sir have there been any thoughts about Narco terrorists?"

Henry Reagen: "Yes, we are looking into that."

WBZ Reporter David Moore: "Mr. Reagen, any satellite pictures?"

Henry Reagen: "Unfortunately no, we didn't have a satellite in that area. But we are looking at footage from prior days. O.K., I'm gonna go and hopefully I'll be back in thirty minutes with more information."

Bill Elderson turning to face the camera: "Charlie, this is the first time we heard anything about terrorism. He said they are looking to see if Narco terrorists are involved."

Charlie Ritz: "Yes and he also said a ballistic missile. There are all sorts of ballistic missiles. He must have meant an intercontinental ballistic missile, if it was on a path to the United States. The Space Station orbits at roughly two hundred and fifty miles above earth and an intercontinental ballistic missile could easily reach that elevation; but it wouldn't take three minutes. But he really didn't confirm that it was a missile. Mr. Reagan didn't dispute that the astronauts said they saw something but that it was not a missile. We are getting word from a number of news agencies, most notably the AP and Reuters that their sources are saying they are not sure what was launched but it definitely was not a missile. Bill stand by. We are going to cut away to our local stations for a few minutes. Ladies and gentlemen, after this station break we will preempt your morning programing so that we can stay with this developing and very mysterious story."

June 12, 2012 – 6:24 A.M. – Thibodaux, Louisiana – Ozema's Morning Café

The summer morning sunbeams are now penetrating the café's dew covered windows. But the early morning routine has been shattered. The polite hushed early morning conversations have erupted into scared agitated chatter and loud declarations. The morning diners are no longer interested in breakfast as they crowd around the three TV's. Everyone has a theory about this mysterious and frightening launch and as usual there are those who must loudly convince everyone to agree with their opinion.

Earth Project Atelier in the Exploratory Center

Master Dakka, with a drunken grin of a smile on a face deeply carved and etched by many hostile suns, paced on stage, exchanging small talk with members of the audience as they file into the small amphitheater. He was in an obvious excited state and ready for the anticipated discourse to begin. He has always been my greatest supporter and has always been interested in my work. Once the most famous bio-archaeologist; Master Dakka is now a devoted mental explorer. The oral examination is open to a select audience, mostly members of the Exploratory Association and members of the scientific community and governing officials. But the questions and my answers will be transmitted so that anyone who has any interest, and most do, can follow every detail. I've done this many times and I am never very comfortable up on a stage answering questions from preeminent colleagues and having to justify some of my work. Then there are the detractors who believe that my project is taking too long or going into the wrong direction and of course pointing out my numerous mistakes. But I know this is a requirement to keep funding for my project. This amphitheater and most of the funding for my project comes from the Exploratory Association and members of the governing council. Master Dakka, barely able to contain himself, marched to the front of the stage and signaled for quiet and for the transmission to begin. Some of the audience was still filing in, but Master Dakka, possessing the earthy look of a peasant with sparkling eyes and wisp of unruly red hair, took command of the stage.

Short in stature, but powerful in voice, Master Dakka roared, "Good day, ladies and gentlemen, welcome explorers and scientist, members of the Exploratory Association and Commissioner Joshua. This is an exciting day, a day that we have been waiting for a long time. You all know that I am a big supporter of Mr. Greeo's work." He turned his short compact body to face Greeo. "Finally we gather to celebrate your life's work and at the same time, pick it apart. In the end, we all hope you have a glorious body of work. Even though I am sure everyone here is very familiar with your accomplishments; I will give a brief version of the history of your work. Your name, your adventure, your project is known by everyone, but I want to introduce you from your very beginning." Master Dakka's weathered face took on a serious expression as he turned to face the audience. "Auspicious members of the committee may I present to you Mr. Greeo8.2. Being a designated 2 he realized at a young age that he would have a future in exploration and science. His father, being designated a 2, took the scientist route and specifically cellular studies. Mr. Greeo naturally followed in his father's footsteps, but combined exploration, adventure, grueling fieldwork and of course, a very good author of his exploits and his passion. His passion has been our universal passion. To find someone, some race, some creature that is our equal; to be our friend, our comrade in this eternal journey through this vast lonely universe. To find a world that has the same restless yearning for meaning that has propelled our experiences. We have traveled far and found that the small part of the universe that we have explored is teeming with life. But most forms of life are on the single cellular level, and when we do find a higher form of life, we find that it is evolving in another direction and would never prove to be a true neighbor. During the one hundred eighth generation, there was a lot of excitement and discussion of creating new life forms that could be a partner with us through the eons of time. Many in the community wanted us to just clone ourselves; a newly perfected process, and then let the clones colonize useful planets. But a small group of scientists, including Mr. Greeo's father, thought it would be wiser for our world if we took a more complex life and shaped it into something similar to us but genetically different. Thinking that one day a need for an infusion of new and different DNA may be a necessity. Others felt the laws of natural selection may prove to be the best way to keep the flame of high-order life burning. During the one hundred eighth generation, many of the theories proved to be unsuccessful; except one promising body of work that was done by Mr. Greeo's father, Greeo7.2. The son took the father's theories, tested only in the laboratory, to different worlds and applied these theories with failure in most instances except for the phenomenal success of the Earth Project. And that is why we are here today. So now I'll ask Mr. Greeo for an opening statement and a short overview. Then the members of the committee will ask questions and give comments. I want everyone to know the significance of this meeting is that members of this committee and the Exploratory Association will vote for continued funding for this project. I also want to advise that not everyone here is a member of the committee and questions and comments are limited to only six committee members. Committee members, please remember to introduce yourselves before your questions and comments. Mr. Greeo knows you well but members of our audience may not, so please a little information about yourself." Master Dakka turned to face Greeo and with a very solemn, serious expression on his face, "Mr. Greeo, this committee and the world await your report."

The amphitheater had sixteen rows of seats with carved walls depicting scenes of exploration. The floor above that opened onto the amphitheater was where Greeo's office and laboratory were located. Parts of the second and third floors of the Exploratory Center were the Earth Project Atelier. Greeo slowly walked stiff legged to the front of the stage. Coarse, short, slightly curly brown-tinged black hair framed the famous handsome face with the hypnotizing hazel eyes and ample stone gray lips. As he walked to the front of the stage he could see the eager smiles from friends and the malicious sneers from his detractors.

"Thank you Master Dakka and I would also like to thank the members of the committee for your past advice, help and continuing support. I began this journey with the study of the cell at its simplest form; first as a student of Master Zee and then at the side of my greatest hero, my father. The amazing cell is the basic structural unit of most life forms that we have discovered. We know about when and how the cell began; but why is still a mystery. We do know everything about the inner workings of the cell. The nucleus of the cell contains the genome; all the genetic material needed for reproduction. The genome is divided into linear DNA, deoxyribonucleic acid, molecules called chromosomes. The sequence of the nucleic acids is the basic instructions for building a life form. The sequence of the DNA contains the organisms' encoded hereditary information and this chain of DNA has over three billion informational codes. We've known this since the fifty ninth generation. We also know that foreign genetic material can be artificially introduced into the cell and genetic codes can be rearranged. Genetic manipulation and rearranging the DNA sequence has been a major part of my work. My father had many theories regarding manipulating life forms and together we tried these theories on many worlds. As we all know it's easy to create life or foster life that is already thriving. There are life-forms throughout the universe. But of course most life forms do not last for long. And what life there is, the vast majority is no further advanced than simple multicellular organisms. The more advanced forms of life quickly become extinct to other forms of more advanced organisms. Natural selection, the strongest survives. The problem has been that when the strongest no longer had any challengers, it began to destroy itself. The challenge was to alter a higher life form- physically, intellectually and socially; so that it had a chance to survive itself. Earth or the Blue Planet as many of you call this planet harbored many interesting creatures, but one, the primate, had numerous impressive characteristics. My Father challenged me to try and modify this life form. And, as you all know I have had enormous success physically shaping this species. My method of rapid enhanced evolution has created a creature in our image. I still have a ways to go but I am close to creating a species similar to us, but with minute critical differences in the DNA. Intellectually you have all witnessed this creature's rapid progress. This has occurred because of the critical modifications to the brain that many of you have suggested—and for that I say thanks. We now have the species developing its intellectual capacity at a rapid pace. Socially, in the beginning, I made very good progress; but now I am at an impasse. I now know that I may have made some mistakes. My experiment is still a work in progress. I truly believe that I am on the right path and I hope you believe likewise. I really believe I will create a neighbor, a friend, a partner that we can depend on to help explore this beautiful universe. Now I will take questions."

Master Dakka slowly stood and asked, "Mr. Greeo, do you need anything before we start the next phase of our meeting?"

The usual fear inducing doubts were already receding. Greeo said, "Nothing, thank you."

Looking into the audience Master Dakka said, "The first member of the committee to probe and investigate your project will be Master Daal."

"Mr. Greeo, members of the committee and the audience, my name is Master Daal, chief explorer of the back half of the first quadrant, the forty fifth to ninetieth sector. Mr. Greeo, it is such a pleasure to be here today. I am so excited about the work that you have done. I find it remarkable how fast you have molded this species into near visual replicas of ourselves. Communication—anyone of the esteem members of the committee—could go to your planet and communicate with almost any of the subjects of the experiment. Again, I say remarkable. I have been following your work with eagerness and excitement. I have no problem with your work. I do have one question about your future plans. The subjects in your experiment, man, as you call them, are an explosion of life. From the moment a few cells are fertilized to their full bloom of life to their eventual decay and death is so rapid. Even for the longest lived subjects; the time span is disappointingly short. Its flame burns so fast. They have a consciousness that could last forever. But they have a body that begins to downgrade so quickly. I think many of their social and behavioral problems could be the result of such a short life span. Is it a disease of the DNA? Does the DNA need artificial material or material from another planet to strengthen it?"

Smiling at Master Daal, Greeo could feel his confidence take over, "First let me thank you for your kind words and the help that you have given me throughout this project. There are many factors and yes the DNA will have to be further manipulated. The telomeres will need to be lengthened and manipulated; also the mitochondrion which provides energy for the cells will have to be reconstructed for more efficient functioning. But there are many other determinants and I will accept any advice dealing with these factors. Gravity is really brutal, but in this environment very necessary. The distance to their sun is so close that the sun's radiation is a life giver as well as a killer of life. It's amazing the amount of bacteria and viruses that is always living on and inside man. This is a major factor in not introducing them to other planets. And now, man is just multiplying so quickly that there is a need for some to die to make room for the new born. I had not expected for them to reproduce in such numbers. But for the sake of the experiment, there is a need for a short life span. The project needs subjects that have a short life span so that we can judge if enhanced evolution has been successful and if we are going in the right direction. What I call the Age of Testosterone is coming to an end; it must come to an end. The brutality and out of controlled reproduction must and will come to an end. I am pretty sure that further manipulation of the DNA can dramatically slow aging, but before I deal with ageing I must deal with the social disasters that I have never been able to get under control."

"As I have said before, I am a supporter of your work," explained Master Daal. "I was fortunate to be allowed to be one of the six members of the committee to question you. But I mostly wanted to be here to let you know that I admire your dedication and passion for this work. Humans become a seed ready to flower in an instant. The flower and the fruits of accomplishment are gone before it can be enjoyed. Each one is a fast burning story and all end with the same last verse, from stardust to stardust. I know you will find a way to slow things down. I understand why your subjects have their regular hibernation; but hopefully you will be able to shorten the extreme lengths of inactivity. Thank you for such good work Mr. Greeo."

"Thank you, Master Daal, for your support. I will slow the aging process but at the moment I need the rapid life span for my study. The brisk life span allows me to see how my DNA manipulation has affected the subjects. Once I have the appropriate physical features, then the immaterial genetic information will survive to be handed down to succeeding generations. I am confident that at the appropriate phase of the experiment, ephemeral humans will come to experience a longer and more vigorous life. The need for sleep is because of the type of nourishment that is necessary during this phase of the project.

Master Dakka rose to introduce the next member of the panel, "Thank you Master Daal. Mr. Greeo, the next examiner is Mr. Shramana 12.1. Mr. Shramana's specialty is socialization."

Dressed in his usual body hugging suit of tiny brown scales, Mr. Shramana placed one hand on his corpulent waist; with the other hand he tugged on his long facial hair and in a shrill voice said, "Thank you Master Dakka and fellow members of the scientific community for allowing me to be on this committee. My specialty is really all of the behavioral sciences. Master Dakka's face blushed a radiant grin after being corrected. Mr. Greeo, I have to agree with Master Daal that man's life is way too short. There is way too much death on your planet. If slowing the age process would do one thing, it may slow down the ghoulish celebration of death. There was a muted laughter from the crowd. I must say I am not a devotee of your work. There is a myriad of serious problems, but I want to focus on one—the God Syndrome."

Greeo knew this was coming; it was always amusing to his detractors. "Ah yes—the God Syndrome."

"Yes the God Syndrome. You have done good work in some areas of this project; but a big criticism of mine is the overwhelming negative effects of this syndrome on your experimental subjects."

"What negative effects?"

Mr. Shramana's shrill voice echoed, "It's all consuming."

Greeo knew this would be a question he would have to answer. His distractor always pointed to this as one of the weaknesses of his project. Greeo smiled and reacted with feigned surprise, "I also believe that there are some negative effects, but there are also many positive effects and many absolutely needed effects. I have explained this in fuller detail in my body of work. But I will try to explain today the why and the how. I believed when I started this investigation, and I still believe, the subjects of my experiment were the best species with the possibility to succeed. When I started working with them they were still animals with only two desires: to feed and to procreate. At first I worked among them and it was only the fears of my powers that kept them from killing one another. I knew that I could not stay on earth forever; and a climate change of frigid temperatures was beginning to have some effects and so help was needed. That's when I started using select individuals to speak for me. I first selected leaders such as Mahavira, Ahura Mazda and Zoraster to speak to the subjects and let them know that they could have free will but with responsibilities. I had other attempts—Moses was another. I've had some success in lessening the barbarism, but these leaders developed a cult following which quickly evolved into individual religions. An unintended effect of all these religions was that they worshiped their creator, which of course is me. When they couldn't explain something they attributed it to their God. My original intent was for peace and harmony. I tried to create laws or commandments that all could benefit from and which would allow the social species to survive. But, so far no religion has worked with this species to the really desired effect. They will respond only to continual visual displays of power. You have to rule with fear. Of course even fear doesn't always work. Fear is not what we want in our neighbors. We have been slowly manipulating the DNA and introduced some mild hormonal changes to reduce some violence. I don't want to eliminate fierce competition because that has a major role in enhanced evolution. I want to keep passions but phase out such emotions as jealousy and greed. Clearly there is much work still to be done. I hadn't expected them to multiple so rapidly. It has been difficult to work with the huge population and religion was a way to deal with the masses. Once I breed out the raging sex drive and the desire to kill, population levels will drop quickly and there will be no need for the mass communication on the primitive level that I am using on Earth."

Waiting to pounce as soon as Greeo stopped speaking, Mr. Shramana snapped, "So on your next mission; what do you plan to do about religion?"

"I think when I return organized humanity will be mature enough to know the truth. They like to belong, with a few exceptions. And even the exceptions are usually psychological; which may be easily fixed. I think that when they are able to see my future plans, they will be very cooperative; most humans crave for a sense of belonging. They will want to be part of the future. Religion won't be necessary when they know their creator. They already realize that many laws of nature have been fine tuned to allow for intelligent life."

Mr. Shramana shifted his bulk to his left leg, passed his hand over his fat wrinkled hairless head and directed his question to the audience. "But, what of the malcontents; you know there will be resisters. What if the malcontents intermix with the cooperatives and learn knowledge that should not be in the hands of a dissatisfied population? Mr. Greeo, I am very much afraid you may be unleashing a very virulent virus-like contagion. These malcontents, with enough knowledge, could create much harm to your cooperatives and ultimately to us. Why not eliminate any subjects of your experiment that are not cooperative? They must be told that immortality, as they know it, does not exist as far as we know. They say that they are made in God's image. What will their reaction be when they find out that image is us?" Shramana smiled at members of the committee after each of his statements. "Who is the creator? Does anyone here know? Who knows the divine order of the world? What will your earth man think when he finds out that we are still debating, if, what they call mathematics, was created by us or is a divine or a cosmic invention that we simply discovered?"

No longer smiling, Greeo looked at Mr. Shramana with a steely emotionless stare. His noble features, with a fine straight nose and smooth light facial skin now look dark and menacing. "Mr. Shramana, in summary, religion and the God Syndrome was created and used because I knew I could not stay on Earth or the Planet Blue as you stubbornly persist on calling it. After I introduced agriculture I knew something or some mechanism would be needed to get the subjects to unify into civilizations and I would not be there to direct them. I introduced religion and the God Syndrome to accomplish this. I used a number of subjects to spread the ideas among the masses. On subsequent visits I conveniently used other subjects to continue spreading these ideas."

Mr. Shramana pointed a finger at Greeo and opened his mouth to speak.

Greeo put out his hand to motion to Shramana not to interrupt him. "Please Mr. Shramana let me finish this short summary. True, when I was busy with other aspects of the experiment, I allowed religion to grow in unexpected ways. When this experiment first began I needed the violence, I needed the environmental challenges, and I needed the chaos so that man would develop in unforeseen ways, so that they were not merely clones of us. I introduced religion when a new phase of my experiment began. I truly believe that my subjects, mankind, when told that immortality, as they know it, does not exist as far as we know; but that I can promise a life that can last tens of thousands of years will then voluntarily cooperate and work hard to help me fulfill the ends of my experiment."

Mr. Shramana smiled then turned from right to left surveying the audience. "Mr. Greeo I know your father and wherever he is in this universe I know he is proud of your work. Mr. Greeo, I wish you success and I will be very interested in your next visit to The Blue Planet. I think there will be many problems awaiting you religion, overpopulation, destruction of the beautiful planet, just to name a few. If you are successful in dealing with these problems, then we may someday have a neighbor and I hope a friend."

Before Mr. Shramana could sit, Master Dakka bolted to the front of the stage, "Thank you Mr. Shramana I think our next examiner is Madame Samara3.3."

Madame Samara was a tiny beauty with delicate facial features and a smoldering gaze. Standing very erect, she locked her gaze on Master Dakka and said, "Thank you, Master Dakka, my favorite mental explorer."

Master Dakka grinned maniacally as he walked back to his seat and was unable to look away from her smile. In fact all eyes were focused on the famous beauty.

"Mr. Greeo, welcome back home. I won't take the time to introduce myself because I'm sure everyone knows I am your most active critic and we have been intellectual adversaries for some time. I dread what my life would be if I didn't have the challenge of repudiating your carnal work."

Greeo always admired her ability to be so polite when she tried her best to destroy his life's work. He had always wondered why a three from one of the oldest families took such interest in his work.

"Mr. Greeo, I'll say today, as I've said many times before, that you are creating a monster. The subjects of your experiment are a replica of us, but only in physical appearance. They are arrogant, narcissistic creatures that are clinging to their boiling rock. They are vicious diseased animals. These animals are cold, heartless killers of all life forms. I think one of the first things that you should have done was to breed out emotions. Some are fearless, confident and charismatic; others are weak, scared loners, but when the time comes all are merciless predators. Men or humans, whatever you call them, have microscopic organisms crawling all over and inside of them. Bacteria, fungi and other microbes live on their skin, in their nose and their intestinal tract. Some of these microbes are pathogens that cause infections. They can never be allowed to leave Planet Blue for fear of infecting anything they come into contact with. Again, I must stress to everyone listening, that Mr. Greeo has created rapidly reproducing killing machines. Mr. Greeo, you are proud because of your subjects' increasing intelligence. They are discovering the greatest tool that you gave them: a brain that may have a greater intellectual capacity than our own brain. Already they have made enormous strides in the field of science they call physics. They are learning how to manipulate physical objects by just using their brain's impulses. What will we do when they learn to travel using the repulsive force of the universe's energy fields? This creation is a highly intelligent killing machine. I say that we should all have *fear of these animals. I will vote, as I have always, to end this project. In all probability man will destroy himself. But if they don't and they continue to progress intellectually, then we should do something to destroy this predator."*

Eyebrows in a downward slant and a slight smile defined his face; he let out a rush of air, and then began his rehearsed counterattack. "Madame Samara, it's nice to see that you are still excited by my project. These millions of microscopic organisms which in most cases are bacteria are needed so humans can survive. Our ancestors roamed this planet with just as many life giving microscopic organisms crawling over and in their bodies. We have been able to alter our bodies over generations that have made most, but not absolutely all bacteria, antiquated for the survival of life. Madame Samara, I know that you are aware that everyone on this planet has the bacteria, solarbacillus, in their eye socket cavity that helps us to convert solar energy into life giving sustenance and to see in many wavelengths. Humans can see in only one wavelength. They are blind to most of the universe. I plan on strengthening man's body in many different ways and one will be to eventually make his body strong and efficient to survive in any environment without the need for these single cell helpers. So eventually they would spread no more disease than we would when we inter a new environment. Yes, they are violent. They are an unusually destructive species. I have not tried to breed this instinct out of them. We have known for generations that out of chaos, out of the need to survive the attacks of other ferocious beast or single celled microbes, viruses, environmental hardships and maybe most of all the treachery of your own species evolves a stronger, smarter and more creative species. Everyone here knows that our own species advanced rapidly when there was such an abundance of challenges and now that we have conquered most of our known challenges our rapid increase of knowledge has slowed appreciably. Some would have you believe that we are no longer advancing at a rapid pace because we have reached the pinnacle of knowledge. I believe there is a whole universe of knowledge waiting for us to discover. I am creating in this species curiosity, restlessness, innovation and the desire for risk taking, to have a restless spirit and the urge to help us push beyond what is known. Madame Samara, if you truly follow my work, you would know that there are huge areas of the planet where there is peace and few acts of violence. Humans are violent and before they can be allowed out of their solar system they will have this destructiveness bred out of them."

Slowly rising from her seat, with a face as inviting as the surface of a cold moon she spoke cautiously, "Mr. Greeo, what of your assistant, the neurobiologist, and his refusal to leave the Planet Blue? It has been recommended that because of the planet's hostile environment, the constant attack by bacteria and viruses and the harsh sun that a stay of one hundred earth-years is the maximum. Your assistant has been bound to that harsh planet for over four hundred earth-years and is seriously jeopardizing his life. His living among the beasts is endangering his life. Everyone in the Exploratory Association and many people in the government are confused about his involvement in this project. He traveled to the Blue Planet to do neural mapping; something that he could have done here at the Exploratory Center with the information that you brought back on your return journeys. Now he refuses to return and is jeopardizing his life for no apparent reason."

A big smile stretched across his face when he thought of his friend Overman. "I wouldn't call Mr. Overman my assistant. He has become a vital part of this experiment. His initial involvement was just his desire for adventure. We have been able to mingle among the masses of humankind as one of them. It is risky, but also very rewarding to observe the subjects on their level. Mr. Overman has been so intrigued by man's struggles, passions, his deficiencies and his complex emotional-social world. He has elected to live among our experimental subjects. In some cases he has been able to steer man's progression into a certain direction."

Madame Samara was still standing, her sculptured pouty lips parted slightly with the ends turning up into an angry smile and her heated stare focused on Greeo. She didn't wait for a break in Greeo's explanation. She shouted, "Mr. Greeo, how has Mr. Overman avoided detection and is it true that he is planning to interbreed with this species and please tell this committee that you will not allow this to happen."

Glaring eyes and a closed mouth smile were Greeo's attempt to intimidate the rude beauty. The socially battle-harden Madame Samara was unfazed by a facial expression. "Every fifty years or so Mr. Overman moves to a different part of the planet. He takes on a new identity; he now calls himself Wayne and has a new occupation. Yes he will breed; in fact he already has taken a mate. And we are eagerly looking forward to the outcome. We are not sure if conception will result; but if it does we may have our new breed of mankind. As you know the offspring receives half of its chromosomes from its mother and the other half from the father; which could result into a super species."

Once again Madame Samara regally stood up, pointed a finger at Greeo and as she turned to leave, shrieked, "Or maybe a monster that will be capable of committing unspeakable horrors and you shall wear that mantle of disgrace."

Quickly walking to the front of the stage with a grimaced smile Master Dakka tried to convey his infectious optimism. "Well Mr. Greeo, Madame Samara's prescient safety concerns are honest concerns. Our next committee member is Sir Kong Zi 9.9."

Kong Zi was small, willowy and delicately handsome and because he was in academia and a devoted researcher, he seldom saw sunlight which was why his skin was luminous and impossibly pale. His long stringy hair, the color of earthly morning sunshine, looked like it had not been groomed in years. His small black eyes and his constant smile radiated a warm feeling. "Mr. Greeo, I asked that I could be on this committee so that I could express excitement on the success of your experiment. I am always amazed how you were able to sculpt your subjects to look almost identical to us. One of your subjects could be sitting in the audience and we would never know. Communication, language, has been an outstanding success. Some of the obstacles that I see are food, taste, emotions, reproduction, religion, the short life span and brain power. I know some of my colleagues have questions concerning these problems, so I will limit my queries to only taste and food. I think I know why you engineered your test subjects to have such a ravenous appetite; but I'll let you explain why your subjects do not receive most of their nourishment from the sun."

After Madame Samara, Greeo was thankful that his old friend and enthusiastic supporter was the next member of the panel. "Sir Kong Zi, thank you for your constant and unwavering support. On Earth, life forms called trees are able to reach large proportions and some can live for hundreds of earth-years with only water, some minerals from the soil and sunlight. They get their energy like most life forms in the universe from stars. But I was seeking a way for man to develop a brain like no other brain in the universe. Man's need to adapt and to be cunning and to be able to feed himself had a large impact on the development of his brain. Human brains now need more energy than what their small bodies can get from the sun. Humans understand about one hundredth of their brain. They have not been able to harness the wondrous creative power of their mind. They will be super beings when they are able to control their brain's abilities. Taste, I had to give them this sensation so that they would have an overpowering addiction to food so that they could feed their developing brain. Enhanced evolution has created a simple, but also an amazingly complex organism. Some day in the future I hope that I can convince you, Kong Zi, to visit Earth to see the wonders for yourself."

"Mr. Greeo, to explore has been a dream of mine and I appreciate your invitation; but sadly I do not travel very well."

Keeping the meeting going at a brisk pace, Master Dakka walked to the front of the stage and introduced the next examiner. "We are fortunate today to have as our next examiner a scientist that knows a lot about everything, Master Zeus Karoo 1.8. We are delighted that you could be with us today."

Descendent from one of the original families, Zeus Karoo towered over everyone in the amphitheater. His firm, calm, old, almost rock-like face was imbued with a sense of authority. "Thank you, my friend, for that introduction. Mr. Greeo, you are a great scientist, the best organic engineer and I must agree with Madame Samara, possibly the creator of a monster. You just said that when your subjects understood the capacity of their brain they would become super beings. I agree with you. You have done such a superb job that they may become more powerful than their creator. Such a powerful creature should have control over

its actions, and Mr. Greeo, we all know that your experimental subjects are capable of unspeakable horrors. We have come into contact
with organism on many planets and none of these organisms committed such heinous acts on members of their own kind as your earth man
does on a regular basis. We have received reports that since your recent
return, horrific wars are occurring on your planet with millions of casualties. I'm afraid if we ever allow your earth-man to escape from his
planet, he would not be a good and appreciative friend but a destroyer.
Their eventual super intellect, their violent tendencies and their out of
control reproduction could eventually become a threat to our society.
Mr. Greeo just their rapidly increasing numbers and their inability to
restrain their reproduction makes these subjects a potential failure. If
you do not check this rapid increase in population, they will destroy
their beautiful planet. Your earth-man acts as if there is an infinite supply of everything. They say every life has value; then they allow a large
portion of the population to starve and to live in unspeakable conditions. If something is not done soon their planet will never recover from
the burdens they are imposing. They are destroying their own planet,
what would they do to someone else's home. Also, why the destruction
of the Red Planet in this system? I am voting for you to return one more
time; to fix the violence and the destruction. But if substantial progress
is not made, I will vote to end the experiment and the extermination of
all of your experimental subjects. It would be too dangerous to allow
them to descend further into the darkness and then eventually escape
their planet."

After Master Zeus Karoo's thrashing of his experiment Greeo felt
at peace; his face shone with serenity. Karoo had just said that he would
vote for his return and if Master Zeus Karoo said he could return he
knew the other members of the committee would vote for his experiment to continue. "Master Zeus Karoo, I thank you for the constructive
critique of my work. Violence, when you have to fight to survive, makes
a creature more creative in ways of survival. As I said before, I wanted
the brain to develop to be resourceful, creative and dynamic. I can turn
off the violence. I can go into the amygdala and the medial orbital fron-
tal cortex of the brain, which are the centers for emotions, and dial up

or down any emotion. Reproduction will be a little more difficult, but it can be fixed and it will be fixed. Once I train a few of their scientists how to fix the emotion centers and to reduce the body's sexual needs, they can then perform these surgeries en masse. Many will volunteer for these surgeries, but millions will refuse. My dilemma is what to do with the refusals. Before my return I will seek the advice of the committee members on what to do with the refusals, the resisters."

Before Greeo could add anything else to his answer and before Master Dakka could make his swift waddle to the front of the stage, Eve Saraswati de Docent; known as the brilliant mind with an intoxicating beauty attached to its exterior, stood to ask the next questions. A member of the highest levels of academia, she stood there in her serene hauteur and hypnotic grace not needing or wanting an introduction. Greeo always felt ill at ease and under-prepared when he was in the presence of her ever-present melancholy smile and her penetrating icy pink eyes. Her usual meticulously arranged bright white hair now hung loosely and windblown messy framing her small sensuous face. De Docent's tranquil but oddly ringing voice commanded all, from students to colleagues to government officials to listen with astute attention. "Mr. Greeo, you are often the subject of my lectures. My students love to debate the greatness of your experiment or the abject failure of your project. I think my lecture theater is a microcosm of our greater world. Members of our society either believe you are the greatest scientist currently adding to our knowledge in all fields or you are a scientist on a silly folly wasting enormous resources. You are probably this era's most famous or most controversial scientist. Words, phrases, and events from your experiment have become part of our normal conversation. You have not only changed the inhabitants of Earth, you have also changed this world. I believe we need more explorers like you. We can never stop learning, and if your experiment would stop today you will have already added so much knowledge to our world. We have invented words and new fields of study because of your project. Because of that I thank you and your father, wherever he may be at this time. I feel that we all owe you a depth of gratitude. Greeo cast his gaze downward so that the audience wouldn't see his embarrassed grin. I know your biography. I know the story of your experiment. I have studied you and your work. But our world does not fully know you. You might not be fully prepared for what I will ask of you; but I hope you will take this opportunity to explain to everyone what you have done and what you plan on doing. I know your project is near its end and really at its most crucial stage. Please Mr. Greeo; give us the history of your project, why you decided on certain courses of action, some of the high points of the experiment and what we can expect in the future."

Greeo blindly scanned the audience, swallowed hard and then gazed downward until he could gather his thoughts. He turned to directly face Eve de Docent and began to talk to her as if she was the only one there listening to his story. "I want to thank the de Docent for those kind words. Before I talk about me and my project, I would like to let everyone know what has happened to my father. As you all know my father was always happiest when he was exploring new worlds, charting the universe. He was never more excited than when he would discover a planet with a friendly environment and then sending back to our researchers, engineers, academia and our whole society new information to study and investigate. He is one of the last of his generation and the burden of age was making it apparent that it was near time for him to extinguish his energy field and to blend with the newer generations. He never had any desire to fade from life and to be part of someone else's experience. He decided that once his energy field was extinguished then he would be no more. My father, at this time is traveling to the frontiers of the known universe. He is traveling in life suspension until he reaches the unknown. Once he reaches his destination he will become aware and capable of sending back data for us to study. He will do this as long as his physical body is capable and then his conscious mind will be able to relay limited information until that too expires. Yes he has chosen to end his field of energy on a distant speeding rock and to expire doing what he has loved doing his whole life. The quadrant of the universe that he wants to explore is the same quadrant in which Earth lies; but of course the frontier lies a great distance from Earth's galaxy. We estimate that on the quindecennial of his departure he will reach the frontier and then we should start receiving data from my father and if he is able to find a sufficient energy force he will start sharing the wonders of the universe with us as he has done his entire life."

"My project started with my father discovering a blue planet. There was much excitement with its discovery; but that excitement quickly waned when no higher life form was found among its teeming masses of life. My father suggested that maybe we would never find a life-form like ourselves since we had been exploring the universe for generations and this little blue planet was the only planet to have such sophisticated and complex life forms. He proposed that we take the life forms found on Earth and create the kind of neighbor that we have been seeking. We decided that we didn't want to create clones of ourselves. We could have done that a few generations ago. We decide through gene manipulation and adaptive evolution to create a life form physically similar to us and intellectual equals with a potential to be superior creating a need for us to continue evolving intellectually. I took on this task not realizing that it would consume a major portion of my life. I ventured to Earth alone and set up a laboratory in a green lush valley. Humans call this area Africa and most now realize that this is where their ancestors originated. I found hominoids on much of the planet that was not covered in ice. I created many species of this hominoid life form; but eventually the need to return to the energy field forced me to set them free to roam and to adapt to their environment in Africa. When I returned and came before the Exploratory Association and members of the government, I met with much resistance and negative opinions regarding my work. Many members of the Association and the Government wanted us to discover a neighbor and not create one; especially a neighbor that might have the potential to surpass us in capabilities. Because of this conflict, I was kept away from my creations for a longer span of time than I had planned. I feared that these species I had created, which had no form of camouflage to hide from their enemies and no armor to protect them, could possibly be extinct. When I returned, I found many of the species had died out, but surprisingly a few species had thrived and began to explore. Yes, they had begun to explore and to adapt to their environment. I moved my laboratory to an island so that I could start working with these hardy species. This was the period in which I genetically modified the vocals so that there could be communication. The first forms of communication were birdlike for some; others grunted and bellowed like the animals that were familiar to them. This was a very complicated phase of the project; to get them to vocalize a sound that would allow them to communicate with me. This also was the period, when, as many of you like to call it, the God Syndrome began. They knew I was their creator, and now they could communicate with each other. When I finally decided on a species that I thought was the most like us and the most capable to survive, it was once again necessary for me to return to the energy field. Earth's sun gives very little of the spectrum needed to survive and gives bursts of life withering radiation rays which makes this planet a less than ideal environment. But this hostile environment has made an incredibly hardy and adaptable species. I have not changed the basic anatomy for the past one hundred thousand Earth-years, just brain manipulation. When I returned, the island and my laboratory were gone and the ice sheets had begun to rapidly retreat to the Polar Regions. The planet is such a young and dynamic ever changing environment. Shifts in Earth's land masses are probably what sunk the island and destroyed my laboratory. My concern soon turned to elation when I found my subjects had survived and were thriving. Humans, my creation, had spread to a large part of the planet. I was surprised at how the species had adopted to the various environments: skin pigmentation, hair structure and color, nostril openings and size were the immediately obvious changes. After careful study I found other various and minor changes. But they were all the same species. What was exciting was that it showed that they could adapt without my manipulations. They went from simple tool use to teaching themselves more advanced agricultural techniques, taming other animals for their use and living in large communities. This was proving all my theories and experimentation on their brain to be correct. I had built a brain that could adapt to a situation and create a better situation. The brain was flexible and ever-changing. The more data they could store, the more rapid they made changes to their environment. Their progress in the past three hundred Earth-years has been remarkable. They are just beginning to understand that their brain is their vehicle and that it has unlimited powers. Their physical bodies will have to be altered to keep pace with brain development; but in another three hundred years they will be able to do this for themselves. My last two expeditions have been mostly observational. My expedition that began about seven thousand five hundred Earth-years ago is the period that many of you call the age of religion. I was so pleased with their advances; but I was also appalled by their vicious violent behavior. I knew this behavior was a result of them having to cope and conquer their environment. I was hoping there would be no need to start manipulating their DNA again, because they were exceeding my expectations in all aspects of the experiment. There had always been the stories and legends of a creator. Much of what they knew about me had been orally passed down each generation. Instead of DNA manipulation I tried reason. At this point I only wanted to be an observer to see how they changed behaviors and adapted. So I chose to contact just a few so they could spread my words and model appropriate behavior. Well, the unexpected happened which occurs often in an experiment. There was an explosion of religions with each having a different method of worshipping their creator, me. The religions have all created laws on what is appropriate nonviolent behavior; but the violence continues. What is most worrying about the experiment is that even the normally nonviolent can, in an instant, turn deadly. My last expedition was for only about fifty Earth-years and mostly as an excited and sometimes very disappointed observer. Their intellectual progress is leaping forward with no boundaries. But the violence continues and the overpopulation is at a critical point. If I am allowed to return; I believe when I make myself known and of course there is no way I could appear on Earth without mankind knowing of my arrival months before I arrived. Their capacity for scanning their part of the universe has increased greatly. I believe with my physical presence and my word, I think I could get the population numbers down to an acceptable level in a few generations. I don't believe I need to use genocidal methods as many of you have suggested. I believe that would only turn a potential friend into a frightened enemy. The destruction of their planet could be halted once I help them discover more efficient and less invasive ways of doing things. I am open to any suggestions or solutions to the two greatest problems: violence and the intake of essential calories. Procuring, then eating flesh is violent. Overman and I are considering working with volunteers and genetically manipulating humans for the last time, creating nonviolent individuals capable of surviving on the sun's energy with a greatly reduced need for their current diet. There will still be a need for high quality protein, but most of that protein could be derived from animal cell cultivation. When they realize they are eating to keep the brain alive and nourished, I believe food will no longer be a pleasure, just a necessity. We will also decrease the levels of certain hormones to lessen their need for incessant, perpetual copulation. These volunteers would be encouraged to interbreed with subjects that were not genetically manipulated. We believe the introduced foreign DNA will be dominant and the favorable characteristics will flourish in the offspring. Because of their brain, the human world is changing too fast for simple genetic evolutionary changes to keep pace. If I am allowed to return, I believe that when I come back to you I will be able to say that we have a friend, a neighbor, and that we are no longer alone in this expansive universe. So my last words to you are: allow me to finish my life's work and when we speak again; if you feel the earth project has been a failure, then I will be in agreement with you for destruction or isolation of the planet. Members of the committee, the Association and the whole scientific community, academia and all that have taken an interest in my project, I thank you for your past and future support. I have appreciated advice in the past and will be grateful for any future guidance for I am only the voice of one. If more detailed information is needed to help you make a decision, every aspect of my project can be found in the public record."

The first applause came from Greeo's greatest supporter, Master Dakka. As soon as Greeo spoke his last words Master Dakka was on his feet, applauding as he slowly walked over to Greeo. The audience applauded but in a subdued expression of support. Master Dakka gave Greeo an enthusiastic handshake and both turned to the audience.

"Mr. Greeo, thanks for being very informative during this inquiry or should I say interrogation. Thank you for being such a preeminent scientist and sharing your knowledge with us. Your work has had a positive impact on our world and I believe when you complete your grand experiment it will have a resolute change on everyone. The return of Mr. Greeo to Earth will be the beginning of the completion of a vision that our world has had for generations. Hopefully the results of this experiment will satisfy our fervent desire to have someone, some contact and not be alone in this cold, vast universe. Remember if you have any questions, all aspects of Mr. Greeo's experiment are in the unrestricted public record and in the communal inventory. Members of the committee, members of the council and everyone else, I thank you for your interest and your commitment to this experiment. I look forward to Mr. Greeo's return."

January 27, 2181---5:03 A.M. ---Thibodaux, Louisiana--- Ozema's Morning Café

Beulah Battaglia slowly walked in front of the ancient building studying its old face. She took a deep sad breath and unlocked the door of the old café knowing that this was going to be the last time she would come before daylight, turn on the lights and, for most of her adult life, start working to get ready for the morning breakfast crowd. Beulah slowly lowered herself into one of the old upholstered chairs, closed her rheumy brown eyes and with every breath she could smell the aroma of coffee, bacon and eggs which had been this buildings comfortable fragrance for two hundred years. The too-thin old woman knew that her marriage to this old relationship was coming to an end. Her deeply wrinkled Sicilian-brown face smiled as she recalled the good times and the various sad occasions. World events had been debated over coffee between these walls for almost two hundred years. Ozema's Café had been created by Beulah's great, great grandmother, Ozema Bergeron, and her sister Pearl. For nearly two centuries five women have owned and operated the café. It was a family treasure that had been handed down from mother to daughter for five generations. The world had changed so much since her great, great grandmother made the first pot of coffee in her café. Much of south Louisiana has disappeared under the Gulf of Mexico; the last super storm, Mingo, did his death dance over the lower half of Louisiana for three torturous days. When it was over a large brackish body of water covered large portions of Terrebonne, Lafourche, Jefferson and Plaquemine Parishes and the uninvited water stayed. Roads, houses, whole towns, churches, graveyards and a culture were permanently underwater. Ozema's Café, which once was over one hundred miles from the Gulf, was now valuable beachfront property. The Café's ability to survive financially from a breakfast crowd was greatly diminished after a large segment of the population retreated from the relentless encroachment of the Gulf waters. Beulah had always thought that her oldest daughter would be the woman to continue the tradition into the next century. But everything in this world has an ending, even tradition. Because the world is in such an unsettled state, because the Gulf of Mexico will eventually eat this land, and because some fool will give an outrageous amount of money for the land, family members want to sell the Café; to end a tradition. The world was constantly changing with long periods of chaos and uncertainty, but Beulah's one consistency was the harmony of the daily ritual of her Café. When the Great Slaughter occurred in the Twenties and Thirties, the breakfast crowds discussed the Muslim War while Sunni and Shiite Muslims massacred each other and when the Chinese nation annihilated their neighbors many thought the United States would soon be involved in an Asiatic war. But the United States was too involved in its Second Civil War to notice the genocidal wars or to even care about the Scourge of Africa, an unnamed and incurable disease, which exterminated most of Africa and much of southern Europe's population. During all the horror and chaos, Ozema's Café was open to serve breakfast even when bacon and sometimes coffee were impossible to obtain. In the midst of the chaos, slaughter, and horror, came a man or a demigod to rescue the world, Wayne and his forty-one children. Surrounded by his tall, energetic, long haired children with identical large somber brown eyes, Wayne was always firm but calm with a presence of authority. With their show of power and the demonstration of alien abilities, they were able to convince the blood drenched world that the mysterious launch in 2012 was a significant event in human history; an event that included the return journey of a creator. His words still ring out, "For the first time in your history you will know who you are and you will be proud, but will he be, when he sees all the death and destruction." This man, this demigod brought peace and brotherhood back to our world. This period of peace and rebuilding is being called the Age of Wayne. He and his children have disappeared; many believe they went back to their home planet, but most think they live amongst us, watching. The last five years have been a period of dread for some, excitement for others and mystical for many, because our telescopes located throughout the world including the orbiting telescopes, and our scientific and mining outpost on Mars, have detected an object in the same sector of the universe that the mysterious launch disappeared into in 2012.This object is moving too fast and on such a defined course that it has been ruled out to be a planet or some other natural phenomenon. Its estimated Earth arrival is 2184. All the excitement and fear of the return of this enigmatic someone or something cannot sweep away Beulah's sadness for losing her family treasure. Whoever or whatever comes in three years will miss his or its chance to hear the early morning polite chatter, the smell of coffee and the taste of a wonderful breakfast at Ozema's Café.

March, 2013

YELLA

"Hello old Friend. I didn't come to you yesterday because a miracle happened. My mind has been racing nonstop. Love and thoughts of bliss have been a continual mental movie. I met someone yesterday. It's been surreal. I went to my monthly appointment and everything was the same as it always has been. It was another mundane Monday like so many other boring Mondays in that dimly lit cherry wood and leather waiting room. I was sitting on my side of the room and everyone else was seated as far away from me as they could possibly get. I had just started reading Justine. The night before, I had finished reading Hermann Hesse's Siddhartha. I was tired of reading peaceful holy stories and had a desire to read a rough and smutty tale. I had barely read the first page of my novel when suddenly the door creaked open letting in a beam of shaded sunlight into the somber waiting room. When she stepped into the beam she was illuminated like an angel. She walked into the room and saw one side of the room was crowded, with some people even standing, and my side of the room as empty as a haunted house. She walked to the nurse's station to check in and then turned, locked her eyes on me, walked into my territory and sat the second chair to my left. My heart felt like it had wings; it was fluttering so fast in my chest. Discreetly I put the book in my coat pocket and sat there uncomfortably just staring at my hands. The angel took a book out of her purse, turned to me and said, "It's such a shame to spend such a beautiful fall morning in a doctor's waiting room."

Those melodious words, that one sentence, and I felt like I was floating. I don't think I have ever felt that kind of excitement. I can't even remember my response or if I even said anything. But then the old fear, my constant uninvited companion started to creep on me and sit on my chest when I noticed that she was staring at me. I turned to face her, expecting to see a look of revulsion or at least shock. But she was smiling and visually examining me. Her face looked small, soft and fragile. She had big chocolaty eyes and long lashes accented by dark eyebrows. My beauty was petite, smartly dressed in a long loose cobalt blue skirt that covered the tops of her polished brown boots. Her wind-blown black hair just brushed the shoulders of her beige blouse unbuttoned enough to take my breath away. I was confused and unsettled when after looking at me she didn't hastily move away from me like everyone else, except the blind and the mentally unbalanced. But she didn't and we spent the next few hours talking. I will tell you more about her later. I've decided to spend every minute of every hour devoted to her needs. I will no longer have time for you my old friend. I know you understand and I know you want me to be happy. I have been keeping a journal since a social worker told a sad and frustrated six year old that he might be able to get out some of his negative emotions by writing. You have been a good friend for the past twenty five years and you occupy a large portion of my closet. I know that when I am gone that no one will want to read a lifetime of thoughts, frustrations and hurts of an insignificant. Dear Friend, I want to close my last chapter with you by summarizing my life in a few pages. Maybe I will let her read the summary so that she understands who I am. Maybe I should forget about the past and have October 17, 2011 as my new birthday and begin a new life. I am worn out by all the excitement. I think I will take a warm bath, have lunch, and get a good sleep so that I can begin my brief biography tomorrow when I am good and rested. Good bye old Friend. I will see you tomorrow."

October 19, 2011   **Wednesday**   **7:00 a.m.**

"Good Morning old Friend. I easily fell asleep last night, but was chased by dreams. Some of the dreams that I can remember were fantastic, but others were dark and fearful. But I am ready to put my life story on a few of your welcoming pages. Thank you Friend, thank you so much and goodbye, for today should be my last day with you."

My Life

I was born August 5, 1981 on an exceptionally hot and humid Wednesday morning at 8:58 A.M. My mother told me that for the last three months of her pregnancy the weather had been brutally hot and muggy. She said that she spent the whole summer in our house to escape the heat. The pregnancy had been normal and the birth had been relatively easy compared to when my brother came into the world; but she said she knew the first time she saw me that something was wrong. The doctors and nurses assured her that everything would be fine. By three months, she said we were seeing doctors on a regular basis. Doctor inspections became a routine that I would keep for the next 18 years. My skin, the whites of my eyes, the edges of my brown pupils, my fingernails, streaks in my hair and my teeth are yellow. Unfortunately, it's not a pretty canary yellow. I would have settled for a bright lemony yellow. Unfortunately my color ranges from a brown-ish jaundiced yellow to depending on the season and sunlight to a sickly greenish yellow. I have always suffered from allergies and when my red rimmed eyes are peering out of my yellow face I can really create a buzz of whispers when I pass by people. The doctors first diagnosed me as having carotenosis. They recommended that my mom should not feed me any carrots, sweet potatoes or carrot juice. By the time I was six years old I was well acquainted with the needle sucking blood out of my arm. A needle in my arm was no longer frightening, it was routine. I was checked for jaundice. My liver, spleen and pancreas have always been a favorite topic with the many doctors and specialist I have seen over the past two decades. They checked and rechecked and checked again for hepatitis or liver cancer and occasionally for pancreatic cancer. I was checked for Mirizzi's syndrome and monocleosis; I was prodded for parasites that can live in the bile duct. That led to the chicken theory that I will discuss later. For about a year the doctors were leaning towards a diagnosis of hypothyroidism. The problem with that diagnosis was that the only symptom of hypothyroidism that I had was yellow skin. I did not have a low heart rate, feelings of tiredness or feeling cold, muscle or joint pain and I was not overweight. My parents spent a small fortune trying to find a definite diagnosis and hopefully a cure. After a decade of seeing every type of specialist, the usual answer we got was a confused shrug of the shoulders. My mom even took me a number of times to see my Taunt Annie who was a respected Treateur. She questioned me about my dreams. When I was a teenager, as a joke, I told her that I had a dream of attending a Black Mass with three witches. She nearly drowned me in holy water. When a diagnosis was never found the attention turned to my poor mother. She had the same test that I had taken plus she was checked for syphilis, cirrhosis and was question extensively about her food intake, her alcohol or drug consumption and habits during her pregnancy. This led to their stupid chicken theory. Chickens are one of the few animals that naturally have some yellow skin. My mother was questioned about her chicken habits. Did she come into contact with chickens while she was pregnant, did she have a chicken as a pet, and did she eat an abnormal amount of chicken while she was pregnant? The result was to make my poor mother feel guilty about my condition. Doctors and their staff usually had sympathy and caring concern for me. The rest of the world had suspicion, stares with laughing whispers, scorn and unfortunately even hatred. My parent's friends stopped visiting because of their fear of my yellow condition. People did not let their children come near me. My brother, Alan, six years older than I, has always hated me. He was embarrassed of me and never wanted to be seen with me. He made me stay in my room when his friends came over so that they would not be reminded that he had a monster brother. Some of his friend's parents would not let their children come to our house. I have never been angry at him; I just always wished I could have been a normal brother for him. When I was very young my only playmate was Teyve. When we played in the neighborhood playground he was teased even more than me. Bullies and their weak followers had harsh words for me but they dared not touch my yellow skin. Their taunts were hurtful, "Get out of our park,

Yella. Hey Yella, do you piss lemonade? Hey freak, why you so yella"
and on and on. But I only had to deal with words; they would hit and
punch Teyve and rip off his little cap that he always wore. I now know
that his little cap was called a yarmulke. They threw rocks at us, but I
was so skinny that they would have had to have the pitch control of a
professional to hit me. Our favorite times were when we played inside
the comfort and safety of my home. Mom thought of all sorts of games
for us to play and then she would get us to take a break from our good
times and have a feast of lemon squash and crust less cucumber sand-
wiches that she had prepared for us. Then on one bleak day, before my
Mom could bring Teyve home, his father stopped by to save my Mom
the trip. When he saw me it looked like someone had punched him in
the face. His head physically went backwards and he grimaced as in
pain. The last time I saw Teyve, his father had a grip on his upper arm
and his feet were barely touching the floor as they sailed through the
front door. My Mom said Teyve's family had moved to another neighborhood, but I knew better. I often try to picture what he must look
like as a grown man. If playing with Teyve was some of my best days,
school was definitely the worse. I was seven years old when I started
school. Mom and Dad knew that it might not be a good environment
for me but they were notified by the authorities that I must start
attending school. I can remember my first day like it was yesterday.
That morning, dressed in my new school clothes and carrying my
brand new leather schoolbag that smelled like shoe polish, I sat on the
front steps waiting for my mother to finish dressing for our scary
unwanted adventure. The fall morning sky was blue grey with a few
nonthreatening dark lenticular shaped clouds that allowed a shaded
sunlight through to create a perfect day to die. I would have rather die
than to go to the certain torture that was going to soon begin. When
mother and I walked into the principal's office the huge man seemed
to shrink after he took one look at me. He knew I was going to be
trouble. I was going to cause the flat tire in his smooth running school.
After exchanging a few words with my mother, the principal, Mr.
Bush, disappeared. When I looked up at my mother's face I could see
her lower lip was trembling, she was worried, and she looked scared.

When Mr. Bush returned, he was with a skinny, mean-looking, older lady. He introduced her as Miss Debra Killing. This woman with a long pinched nose, threadbare black hair greased back into a pony tail, pale skin and pencil thin legs was going to be my teacher. She didn't seem to notice my yellow skin. She just looked like she couldn't wait to take me to a closet so she could kill me. Before I left to go with my future murderer, my mother knelt down to give me a big hug. I think she was crying. When I followed Miss Killing into the classroom, my legs were so stiff with fear I could barely walk. Standing in front of the class, I was waiting for the firing squad to come in and execute me. When Miss Killing introduced me to the class I didn't hear my name. I didn't hear anything; I just saw twenty one pairs of eyes staring at me. As soon as I sat in my assigned chair, Shuggie Atkins, a future tormentor, raised her hand. When Miss Killing acknowledged her she loudly said, "Why does he have to sit next to me?" Before Miss Killing could respond a number of students said under their breath, but loud enough for most to hear, "He better not sit next to me." Miss Killing didn't respond to the question. She instead told everyone to open their math textbook. Shuggie said loud enough for all to hear, "My mother won't like this." By the end of the week I was sitting in the last chair pushed into the corner at least ten feet away from the nearest student. Every time I was moved to another chair, a parent would call to complain. Lunch and recess were the worse. Students refused to sit near me at the lunch table. They said I was gross and I stunk and that I made them too sick to eat which resulted in more parents calling to complain. During recess I stood up next to a wall staring at my feet while older kids passed by hurling insults and making jokes about my appearance. When we were told to pass our papers to the front, Sammy the fat stupid kid refused to touch my paper. He told me to put in on the floor so that he could push it to the front with his foot. When Miss Killing angrily told Sammy to stop acting so foolish, he told her that his mom said that he was not to touch Yella. He was not to touch anything Yella had touched or to drink out of the same water fountain as Yella. Some people dream of having the gift of seeing themselves as others see them. I was born with that gift; people had no problem telling me how they saw me. This horrible ordeal lasted until Christmas. I told my Mom the only Christmas present that I wanted was to be allowed to stop going to school. This has brought out such horrible memories that I feel exhausted from the pain. Old Friend, I must stop for today."

October 20, 2011	Thursday	8:00 a.m.

"Good morning my friend, I've just eaten a great breakfast of fried eggs, sausage, fluffy biscuits, French toast and my fabulous coffee. I am so excited because tomorrow is the big day, my first date with my new love. Well, let me get started where I left off yesterday."

As I was saying, school was a horrible torment. I prayed the whole Christmas Holidays for a miracle. I concentrated so deeply in my mental conversations with God that mother thought I was sick. I prayed to God. I begged him. I reasoned with him to change my life or at least explain my life. Was I another Job, was I a changeling or did the devil have his hand on me? My Taunt Annie would always laugh and say that I was just a will-o'-the-wisp that took on an intelligent physical form. Any explanation of why or of what path I should take would be a relief. But I prayed the hardest for a substitute to school. The Holidays came to an end and of course there were no answers or change in my miserable life. On my first day back to my Hell-on-Earth I soon found out that my prayers had been answered. So many parents had complained about my presence in the classroom that I was promoted to a special education class. I was so happy; I was elated. The special education class was for mentally and physically handicapped students. I fit in perfect with this group. The other students in my class didn't care if I was purple with pink pinstripes. Many of them couldn't even name the color of my skin. But the important thing was that they liked me and they didn't torment me. At first my Mom and Dad were not pleased, but relented when they realized that I would not be tortured by the school meanies and that I had an excellent teacher. Other than my parents, she was the first adult to treat me as a person of worth. She had no fear of my yellow skin. She was the person that taught me that the world could be cruel, but there were ways to deal with the harsh realities of life. She was an excellent teacher of math and English, art and music; but her biggest contribution to my education was to teach me to respect and to like myself. She was not just my teacher; she was my guide to live a life of self-worth. Ms. Sally was God's answer to my prayers. I have never asked him for anything else and I still tell him of my appreciation for sending help when I most needed it. For the rest of my first school year I felt safe, secure, protected and I was a willing and eager student. But that reprieve was only for five months. The rest of my school career was hell but I had learned to cope. I had learned to be an island of self-strength. But at the age of sixteen I could legally walk away or I should say walk out of the bowels of hell. My intentions were to find employment and become self-sufficient. But where does a yellow man find employment? I had no chance of being hired for a job that required any human contact or contact with their food, clothes or even their pets. I was an untouchable. I finally got a job with the sanitation department. I was hired to work on a garbage truck on the early morning or late night shift when it would be too dark for people to see my yellow skin. I was so proud that I finally had a job and would no longer be a dependent; now I could be a man. My Mom and Dad showed reserved excitement; they were happy for me, but sad. My young body quickly adjusted to the toil of working on a sanitation truck. Jump onto the back of the truck, then jump down, haul a heavy garbage can to the truck, then jump back on to the truck was the routine done over a hundred times in a shift. It was a body beating workout that I learned to love. The smells emanating from the cans could be gagging. The number one rule was not to get any garbage juice on your clothes, because that smell would chase you for the rest of your shift. I loved my job; I was on the streets for the first time in my life seeing areas of the city that I did not know existed. I liked the hard work and I enjoyed the fruits of a paycheck. But as usual all was not well. Most of the other workers were black men; a people that complained that the world was prejudiced towards them because of their skin color. It was ironic that they were some of the most vicious people condemning me for my skin color. They wanted someone to be lower than them on the social hierarchy. The job lasted six weeks. One morning dressed in my garbage stained clothes with gloves and a hat that covered most of my yellow skin, the foreman informed me that my garbage truck days were over. My garbage collecting colleagues didn't want me to work with them. They threatened to quit because they felt insulted and disrespected to be forced to work with Yella. I was devastated. People would not even allow me to pick up garbage. This depressing event did produce some good in my life. My Dad stayed up all night talking to me. We sat in his workshop just randomly talking about my life, his life, our dreams, man's weaknesses and his strengths. When the morning sky began to lighten my Dad left to shower, shave and put on fresh clothes. Before he left for his job he came back to his workshop, kissed me on the forehead, enwrapped me in a close hug and said, "Son, I love you." and then with a melancholy smile on his face left for a day of work. In our night-long discourse we discussed different occupations and their merits for a healthy, happy and rewarding life. We also discussed a man or a woman's moral obligations to human society. That's how I decided to become a memoirist. I would write a treatise on isolation. How a person could live within a society and because of certain circumstances is forced into isolation. I would call my work, Chronicles of a Yellow Man. My work became my friend and what started as a soliloquy has now become a monologue that keeps a friendship alive. My Dad built me a small apartment in our back yard so that I could work in private and over the years I have contemplated, meditated and wrote in earnest. I had kept a journal since I was six years old, but I would now write with a purpose. I would write so that our society could see and feel what it's like to be on the outside looking in. I started my work before the age of home computers. When I started writing, no one would have thought to put those two words together, it wouldn't have made sense to say home computers. The computer hasn't really made writing any easier; but it has provided me with innumerable windows to the world. Because of my computer I have realized that I am not alone. I haven't found another yellow person; but I've found thousands of isolated and hurting souls. As the years ticked away, first my Dad died and Mom, who always tried to protect me, died three years later. My brother, Allen, who rightfully hated me, because we could never be a normal family, came for the reading of the will after Mom died. When the will was read and Allen realized that my parent's house and most of their savings had been left to me, his face turn into a snarling beast. I could feel the heat from his face when he wordlessly stared into my eyes inches from my face; he then turned and walked out of the lawyer's office and out of my life. In the will, my parents explained that because of my condition, I would need more help. Most of Allen's life I needed more help; I can understand his hatred. After my parents died, my life, for years, became a routine of writing, thinking and of course T.V. One day in the late summer of 2005, I received a letter from the local prestigious L&M Research Center. This famous research center created by the genius researchers, Dr. Landry and Dr. Mire wanted me to participate in a genetics study. They knew about me because when I was seven years old my Mom had brought me to the Center to see if they could help me. As I remember, they seemed really excited to study me. I spent three years taking blood tests, skin tests, I.Q. tests, emotional stability tests and so many more. I don't know why we stopped going, but now a letter was asking me to return. When I met with the research team, they informed me that they wanted to continue studying my condition, but at the genetic level. So for the last six years, and seventy-six office visits, I have gone to the Center every first Monday of the month to give blood, skin, and hair, to be injected, x-rayed or to lie on an MRI table. I have been a willing lab rat; I enjoy the attention, the social interaction with the team. When a member of the team touches me, holds my hand or smiles I feel a delirious high. My backbone seems to loosen up, my feet are lighter and I can't stop grinning. On the morning of my monthly appointment, I leave when the sky is still dark, walk briskly to the Center, and arrive there at six thirty. I usually sit on a bench that stays in the deep shadows until the Center's doors open at eight o'clock. I always sit along the wall opposite the waiting room door. I want new patients to see me as soon as they walk in, so that there is no uncomfortable surprise for anyone. From my vantage point, I can see the parade of nefarious characters that spill into the waiting room. The Center does all sorts of research; so I am not the only freak that they want to study. For six years many of these characters have been my constant companions in that dimly lit leather and wood waiting room. Since there is no T.V. and very few magazines, many of my companions sit quietly staring at their hands or walls, occasionally sneaking a peek at each other and instantly turning an ear to catch any silence killing conversation. I usually bring a book, but my favorite time- consumer is to visually exam my fellow research subjects. Many other characters have appeared once or twice and are never seen again. Were they too normal? Was it death or were they just too stupid to find their way back to the Center or were they locked up in jail, a mental institution, the zoo. Adrian was one of those temporary visitors. He was the Vincent Van Gogh of the motley group. He always talked, but to the whole group and no one in particular. He always seemed self-satisfied with his remarks about our little world. I once spied him drawing intently and occasionally staring at me. When he was called from the waiting room, he leaned towards me and said, "Here you go, Yeeelaaa." The drawing he handed to me is still one of my favorite possessions. He pencil drew a flattering portrait of me in black and white. I was surprised to see my face in any color other than yellow. I usually had my side of the room all to myself. The other characters were never rude; I just presume they stayed away, like everyone else, because they were afraid that they would catch my affliction. They probably thought that they had enough problems without suddenly turning yellow. The regulars talked among themselves but rarely spoke to me. We eyed each other and smiled from across the room. Some of the regulars could be very amusing and entertaining. Banjo Billy, waking from his walking comatose state, would suddenly pluck at imaginary banjo strings and simultaneously voice his rendition of banjo music, then silence His sleepy Buddha eyes never focused on anyone but he could suddenly focus on some far-off mirage of a thought. With his close cropped black hair, sun darkened face and ninth-month belly; Billy could almost pass for the Holy Man. But my favorite waiting room companion was Judy Jiggles. She was so fleshy, that when she walked hoops of flesh encircling her waist jiggled. Her thighs, always encased in nylon, made a swishing sound when she barreled through the room. She may not have taken good care of her body, but she made sure her face was always meticulously painted. Her makeup hid any facial imperfections, but it could not hide the roll of blubber encircling her neck. She never spoke to anyone; her focus was always pointed to heaven or maybe just the uninteresting ceiling tiles. You could tell she was as frightened of Banjo Billy and a few of the other characters, as she was of my yellow skin. I always enjoyed focusing on her and just when her curiosity forced her to take a peek, her eyes would dart to me. Caught she would refocus on her mediation to the almighty ceiling tiles, but now with a giggly smile on her face. Then there was Miss Kitty Chingalinga. She always had a big crazy, crooked smile on her face with brightly rouged cheeks and always wearing a brightly colored huge free flowing tent dress. Sometimes her gaudy colored dresses were so long, so huge, it looked like she was wearing her own flag and at other times they were scary short. She provided the most waiting room action. Miss Kitty wore mountains of jewelry and when she undulated into the room, a brass jeweled orchestra played the clanking tune of Ching Chinga Ching. On lighter days she sounded like a walking wind chime. Everyone would laugh or snicker when every ten minutes she would loudly complain about not being seen at her appointed time and then with a look of exasperation, her hands in the air and in a loud guttural growl, "There ain't no rest for the weary". She attempted conversations with everyone except me. She never got angry when others ignored her attempts of being friendly. Occasionally she would talk at me, but never an invitation for a conversation. The few times I tried to respond, she would just turn to the nearest seat mate and start or try to start a conversation. My voice never penetrated her costume jewelry defense. I still enjoyed listening to her drivel. Once, when asked what type of work she did; she answered a dog beautifier. It took me a week to realize what she meant. Mr. Gaston Picou was the most frightening and I believe, potentially the most dangerous of my companion freaks. His cap, his shirt, belt, pants, socks and shoes were all desert camouflage.

His camouflage shouted his existence. Everyone took quick nervous glances at Mr. Picou; no one wanted him to sneak up on them. He had a world class stare with absolutely no manners. He would lock on to someone and visually investigate them down to the cellular level. He once told Miss Kitty that he was an algolagnic. Miss Kitty's response was a huge smile and a nervous laugh. After finding the definition of an algolagnic, my skin would crawl when the eyes in the skull would peruse my body. Miss Helen was beautiful. She was the pretty ice queen of the waiting room. Whenever anyone sat or stood near her she would shoot the person a giddy-up stare and if that didn't work she would then wave away the person and say, "Leave, deliver me from your presence". Her dramatic arm action or stance with her chin almost on the same level as her nose made her absolute fun to watch. My colleagues-in- waiting would do little things to aggravate her so that we could hear her semi Queen's English mixed with a little Cajun inflection. I think she was a pretty girl from Chackbay putting on airs. Once she went to the restroom and came back with toilet paper trailing from her shoe. From that day on, Miss Chingalinga always referred to Miss Helen as the poopedoo girl. Michio had already been a regular at the research center when I started back with the study. He was a definite Elvis-want-to be and a pretty good replica. If he could sing; I could be his manager and happy and wealthy we would be. Miss Kitty loved having Michio talk to her. She would sit with a huge smile and sweat dripping from her forehead. When he wasn't around, she would refer to him as her Romeo. One day we all froze in fear when he took from his boot the jewel encrusted derringer and with his appropriate swagger walked over to Miss Kitty so that she could give her swooning opinion. There were villains and saints in that waiting room and most of the time it was hard to decide who the maniac was and who was an innocent. Hooligans and trolls, I loved them all. This was my social life. Then of course the fateful day- Monday, October 17, 2011, that flooded my soul with celestial joy. After my love uttered her first words we never stopped talking. Her ability to converse and smoothly switch to different topics, never lacking for a relevant thought or appropriate phrase or word, made her appear intelligent and cultured.

Her smoky voice never tired. She glowed from an inner fire and this
aura of well-oiled ease surrounded her. Soon her charisma wrapped
itself around me in a warm safe embrace. If I didn't answer a question
quick enough or if I didn't know how to respond she just flowed with
an aristocratic mien to another thought. When she moved to the seat
right next to me, her body heat made my skin get toasty warm. I could
even smell her warm minty breath peak out of the cloud of her exotic
perfume. For most of our time together she had a rapturous expression, but occasionally, for no reason, her pretty mouth would go thin
and crooked and she would look, away with her eyes betraying a
haunted tortured thought. All of our waiting room colleagues stared
in open mouth shock. My associates were as mesmerized as I. I quickly
became besotted with her and was surrounded by this cloud of happi-
ness. After about thirty minutes of nonstop bliss; she suddenly stuck
out her hand and said, "By the way, my name is Millicent, but you can
call me Millie." I quickly embraced her small pale hand with battered
fingernails and said, "It's nice to meet you, Millie, my name is Ye."
Before I finished introducing myself, a research assistant walked into
the waiting room and said, "We're ready for you, Mr. Wayne." Millie
smiled, curled her hair around a finger and said, "Mr. Wayne .... Mr.
Wayne why don't you wait for me and we can go to the Venetian and
get a cup of coffee." With uncontained enthusiasm and a smile frozen
on my face I foolishly giggled, "Oh yes, I'd like that and you can, I
mean it's OK, everyone calls me Yella." Yella was a sobriquet that had
stuck and it was how I saw myself. Millie smiled, "I'll see you in a little
while, Mr. Yella." We did go to the Venetian and we each had two cups
of coffee and it was just a glorious experience. I remember one of the
riddles she teased me with. Conformity, what was once a working
man's protection and now is used by everyone for comfort? When she
saw that I had no idea, she gave her first hint. Worn by workmen in the
Forties; rebels in the Fifties; the uniform for the kids in the Sixties; no
longer just for the poor and the rebels, by the Seventies and Eighties
they had created another obedience to the fashion trend. I was still
confused. She patiently gave what she called her can't-miss hint. She
said that, at first, you could only get it in blue, but now it came in a

rainbow of colors. But different shades of blue were the dominant color. You could get it in light blue, dark blue, used blue, new blue, gray blue, black blue, faded blue, almost-white blue, navy blue, bleached blue, distressed blue, and acid washed blue. As soon as I answered that riddle, she asked what was the name of the monkey that held his hands over his eyes and refused to see and who were the other two monkeys? Heck, I didn't even know they had names. It was her idea to meet early Friday morning at the Research Center. She had a very early appointment and then she said we could have a picnic for lunch. My Friend, My Friend this is it, this is the end. I can no longer lean on your broad shoulders. I cannot thank you enough for your patience. I need to prepare for tomorrow; so with an eternal adieu I take my leave.

Oct. 21, 2011   **Friday**   **9:15 A.M.**

Hello my friend, I'm back. It's a dark horrible day. My life is back to zero or maybe it's over. The shadows have wrapped their arms around me again. How peaceful life was without love. When the fat moon was still smiling I left the house early and in love. When I got to the Research Center I went to my usual dark secretive lair, sat on the cold metal bench and waited for the Center to open. In the deep darkness created by the surrounding dense foliage the metal bench was hidden from view but had a line of sight on the steps leading to the Center's front doors. I sat hidden in the deep darkness, as I had done innumerable times before, and contently waited. I was in love and felt invincible. I felt as strong as Shadrach walking out of Nebuchadnezzar's fiery furnace. At seven fifty, sunlight was barely penetrating the early morning mist, and then suddenly I saw my angel slowly and laboriously walking up the steps. I instantly sensed something was wrong. I stepped out of the darkness and called her name. She froze and slowly turned to face me. My beauty was wearing what looked like a faded red robe and a black mantilla was covering her head and shoulders. I walked a little closer to her and waved her over. She slowly walked in my direction, her eyes deeply sunken and dark, stared in unrecognition, and her pale blotchy face looked fatigue; something was dreadfully wrong. Then my world collapsed when she growled, "What the hell you want?" I said, "Come sit with me" then turned and walked into the darkness. She cautiously walked to the edge of the darkness and with a bewildered expression said, "Listen, I can't remember your name, but I have an appointment inside." I could see from the darkness that her beautiful face looked life-beaten and worn. I stayed in the shadows, but stepped closer and softly said, "Millie, its Yella, remember our picnic." She coughed out a laugh and gave an angry thin white lipped grin and said, "Look you idiot, I won't be eating today and I certainly couldn't stomach food while looking at your pus colored face." My yellow hand swiftly punched into the misty daylight and gently rested on her shoulder, then from the shadows I asked, "Millie, what's wrong. Do you have a problem? Let me help you." Millie swung her fist to knock my hand off of her shoulder, pulled away and with an enraged demonic glare shouted, "Yeah I got a problem and it's you. You freak. You stupid circus freak. You infected abscess of a man. You even smell like an infection." I bolted from the darkness and one yellow hand grasped the back of my beauty's head and my other yellow hand covered her mouth to stop the cringe inducing insults. "Millie stop this. I want to help you. I want to love you. Just say the word and I'll be your Prince and take care of you." She violently twisted, pushed and pulled away, then with a savage smile and eyes pulsating in their sockets she spit out the words. "Prince! Yes I'll call you Prince Sewage, you diseased freak." Without a conscious thought, my hands flew to her throat and tightened to stop the verbal knife attack. Like a damned spider I pulled her into my web of darkness and when she stopped struggling I sat her down on my cold bench. She slouched on the bench and her bluish pale face looked at peace. I sat next to her and asked her what had happened, why didn't she let me help her? I wanted to take care of her every need. I wanted to hold her. I wanted to be loved. There was no response to my pleas. As Millie sat there in a messy pile, with her head slumped to the side, I knew there would be no response. There never will be a response. I sat quietly with her for a few more minutes, with thoughts of attraction and repulsion, racing through my mind. When I decided to leave I knew I couldn't leave her in her current slouching crumbled pose. I gently stretched her into a laying position on the bench. I put her feet on the bench and placed one hand under her head and then I covered her face with her mantilla. My last view of my beauty was of an angel peacefully sleeping in the deep dark recesses of a garden paradise.

My Friend, help me. Help me to be empty again.

January 28, 2012

Made in the USA
Lexington, KY
13 November 2014